Jesus

Embraced

Parenting

helping our children grow spiritually

a relational Bible study

Eric and Amy

Lorenzen

Reader ▲ Hill

Published by
Reader Hill
PO Box 490
Yucaipa, CA 92399
readerhill.com

Reader Hill logo and colophon are trademarks of Reader Hill.

Jesus Embraced

Bible studies to bring us closer

jesusembraced.org

Table of Contents

Jesus
Embraced
Parenting

helping our kids
grow spiritually

Introduction

Hi there, our names are Amy and Eric and we are normal parents trying to raise our kids to become successful Christian adults in a modern world. We love being parents and often it's fun but it's not easy, which is probably the same story for you. We wrote *Jesus Embraced Parenting* to help all of us (including ourselves) raise kids that are spiritually strong, kids that have integrity, compassion, and curiosity. We want our kids to realize how much Jesus loves them, and hopefully they will love him in return.

We don't know you yet, but we will assume a few things about you:

1. **You are a parent** (that title includes bio-parents, adoptive parents, step-parents, grandparents, and folks who have a parenting role in a kid's life -whether there's an official title for you or not)

2. **You are a Christian** (or at least a friend of a Christian) who wants to raise your kids with moral values.

3. **You want your kids to succeed**. The very fact that you are even considering this book says that you want your children to grow spiritually and prosper in their life.

We (Amy and Eric) will try not to make too many more assumptions about you, but we hope you'll enjoy *Jesus Embraced Parenting* and that it will inspire and challenge you to do even better at one of the most important roles you have in your life.

What is this book about?

This book is a **10-week Bible study experience** that is meant to be *done*, not just read. Yes, you will read and answer serious questions, but you will also put God's truth into action. This study includes experiences that help all of us actually do the stuff we're learning about- and that helps us all become better parents. Going through *Jesus Embraced Parenting* will be a commitment because this is not a *quick read*. What you are starting is:

1. **A study about nurturing the *fruit of the Spirit* in our kids**: Galatians 5:22-23 talks about the spiritual fruit that ought to be in everyone's life and we (Amy and Eric) thought that would be a good foundation for a study about parenting.

These nine fruits are love, joy, peace, patience, kindness, goodness, faithfulness, gentleness, and self-control. Each week we'll look at a different fruit and how we can encourage that trait in our kids' lives.

2. **A study about showing and telling**: The first 9 chapters of Proverbs are words of wisdom from a dad to his son. The Proverbs dad says some profound things, although some of the word pictures might not fit our modern society. In Proverbs 4:11 he tells his son the following: "I instruct you in the way of wisdom and lead you along straight paths." (NIV) He instructs and leads; he's telling and showing. That is what we hope all of us will do with our kids: teach them what's right and also model it for them. We should all be show-and-tell parents.

3. **A study that's better done together**: We have found that we are better parents when we can lean on others for support and wisdom, which is why this book is designed to be done in a group setting. You can definitely do this study by yourself, but we think it is far more meaningful when you gather with others and go through this journey together. Please consider doing this with your spouse, a group of friends, neighbors, family, or a church small group.

Welcome Gathering

Get to Know the Jesus Embraced way

At **Jesus Embraced**, we believe that there is great joy and soul-satisfaction in following Jesus. We craft Bible studies that are intended to bring people closer to Jesus and to each other.

Each unique Bible experience is meant to

- Draw you closer to Jesus through His Word and prayer
- Encourage you through friendships among the group
- Empower you with the Holy Spirit's presence and guidance
- Press you with tough questions and real-life situations
- Exhort you into being more of a *doer* and not merely a listener
- Revive your love for the Lord

Our studies are written to be highly relational and scripturally-based, where you'll gather to learn, share, and actually *do the stuff* of the faith.

We trust the Holy Spirit will guide and empower you as you go through this adventure. Thanks for joining in and please know that you've been embraced by Jesus, so embrace Him in return and invite others into this divine hug.

What's Ahead?

If you are doing this study led by a group leader, then during today's gathering your facilitator will explain more details about the weekly gatherings and daily readings.

(If you are a facilitator, please see the book *Jesus Embraced Parenting Group Leader Guide* for directions on leading your group.)

If you are doing this study alone, please realize this is meant to be done over 9 weeks, with five daily readings per week. You can go through the study at a faster or slower pace, but take the time to consider each week's topic before going on to the next.

Respect and Confidentiality

Parenting isn't easy. Every one of us has sinned as a parent. All of us have made mistakes. There is no perfect formula for this. Even if you figure out the best way to parent one kid, the next one will probably be completely different. There is no such thing as a perfect child and there certainly isn't any perfect parent among us.

Because this is a messy process, all of us need to be forgiving and kind toward ourselves and the others in the group. We encourage sharing of struggles and successes. You might hear some painful stories, but please keep those in the group. We ask that each participant in this group agree to keep what's shared in the group confidential.*

The group's facilitator will ask you to sign a Confidentiality Pledge* to make sure you understand the importance of respecting the group and what's shared.

(* Please Note- the Confidentiality Pledge does not pertain to any knowledge of child abuse or self-endangerment. Such illegal or harmful practices will need to be shared with law enforcement for the safety of the child or your own safety.)

Getting to Know your Group

Your facilitator will now lead your group in some getting-to-know-you activities, including some time to share about yourself and your family. (Be ready to share your name, your kids' names and their ages/ grade level, and maybe a fun fact about your family.)

Welcome Gathering
Notes

Confidentiality Pledge

This *Jesus Embraced Parenting* study is meant to be a safe place to share about life, mistakes, and struggles. We want everyone to have the freedom to talk about the challenges of being a parent. In order to create safe place for sharing, we ask that each participant in this study to agree to the Confidentiality Pledge below.

I agree to keep everything shared by my group members confidential* at all times. I agree to uphold the maxim: "What is said in the group, stays in the group."

Name _____

Signature _____

Date _____

(*Please Note- the Confidentiality Pledge does not pertain to any knowledge of child abuse or self-endangerment. Such illegal or harmful practices will need to be shared with law enforcement for the safety of the child or your own safety.)

Jesus
Embraced

Bible studies to bring us closer

The Fruit of

Love

But the fruit of the Spirit is **love**, joy, peace, forbearance, kindness, goodness, faithfulness, gentleness and self-control. Against such things there is no law. (Galatians 5:22-23 NIV *emphasis added*)

What is Love?

Perfectionism vs. Perfect Love

Amy: Unlike Eric, I come from a long Christian heritage, at least on my father's side. I have the written prayers from my great-great grandmother that were for her descendants to come. My grandfather was a WWII pilot who became an entrepreneur in the religious broadcasting field and eventually ended up as a fundraiser for Multnomah School of the Bible. My father and his sister attended a Christian boarding school with the daughters of Billy Graham and other kids of famous Protestant leaders. I was dedicated, along with my cousin, by a nationally-known pastor who was the personal friend of my uncle. It sounds like a great pedigree, but along with that comes the sin that traps so many believers: perfectionism and trying to keep a certain image. Perfectionism goes against godly love. While God's love is freely given, perfectionism demands certain behavior from you to even be accepted, let alone loved.

As an adult, it was hard to accept the life I actually had when I was striving for the perfect Christian life that seemed modeled for me. I thought I had to earn love and acceptance by acting a certain way and leading a particular life. Even after I married Eric and had my first child, I struggled with perfectionism and trying to keep up a "Christian" image. That was very hard because we weren't your typical household: I was the main breadwinner while Eric (who had been laid off) stayed home with our boys. I wondered if others would love and accept us, especially in the church where many taught it was the woman's place to be in the home. I couldn't pretend to be the perfect Christian wife and mom when I obviously wasn't. I was a working mom. Would others be okay with that?

I thought God expected me to behave a certain way and do my life the right way. It felt like I wasn't following "God's rules" and I suspected that he wasn't happy with me. Maybe he wasn't proud of me because we were breaking the unspoken rules of Christian roles. It was hard to feel his perfect love when I was struggling with perfectionism.

Twisted Mindset

Many of us struggle at trying to live up to an image, and that interferes with our understanding of love. We work so hard pursuing something we'll never attain, missing so much that God is offering to us right now.

We can also demand perfection from our kids, which will likely alienate them from us because it's hard for them to see our love for them. Our demands can also really mess up their understanding of God and his love.

Perfectionism can warp our love for our kids and our love for God. Perfectionism will exhaust us, because we are never good enough. Our kids are never good enough. We think love and acceptance is something to work for, to earn. But that's not what love is.

The antidote for perfectionism is refocusing our thoughts on Jesus, who models what true love looks like.

Jesus is Love

We need to understand love and how to practice love because the Bible tells us that love is the core characteristic and motivation of God:

> "Whoever does not love does not know God, because God is love."
> (1 John 4:8 NIV)

If we don't love we don't really know God. Wow, that raises the stakes tremendously. Some things in our Christian life are optional, but love isn't. Without love, we remain ignorant of God. In addition, our children need to know and practice love too, if they really want to know God.

Let's look more into what love looks like, so that we know if love is really active in our lives.

Love Traits

The Bible provides an interesting list of traits that belong to love. Some are obvious to us, but some we normally wouldn't think of as a love trait.

> "Love is patient, love is kind. It does not envy, it does not boast, it is not proud. It does not dishonor others, it is not self-seeking, it is not easily angered, it keeps no record of wrongs. Love does not delight in evil but rejoices with the truth. It always protects, always trusts, always hopes, always perseveres. Love never fails."
> (1 Corinthians 13:4-8 NIV)

Fill-in-the-Blanks

Eric: When I was a kid I would sometimes play word games that were fill-in-the-blank stories called Mad Libs, where you would ask a friend to tell you random words and you would write down their answers. It was meant to be funny because of the bad fit of the words picked. You might ask the other person to tell you an *animal* or a *person's name* or an *adjective* or some arbitrary *verb*. Those words were filled in and then the story was read aloud to much laughter, because it sounded so ridiculous.

Daily Response

1. Replace the word "love" with Jesus's name. 1 Corinthians 13:4-8 is sort of a fill-in-the-blank story too. You can fill in Jesus' name for each of these traits and you will find that it fits. Nothing to laugh at, since His name easily slides into place. Jesus is patient, he is kind, and so on. Since ***Jesus is love***, His name can easily replace the word "love" in each sentence and it still makes sense. See for yourself: try Jesus' name in each blank below:

Love Traits

_____ is patient.

_____ is kind.

_____ doesn't envy.

_____ doesn't boast.

_____ isn't proud.

_____ doesn't dishonor others.

_____ isn't self-seeking.

_____ isn't easily angered.

_____ keeps no record of wrongs.

_____ doesn't delight in evil.

_____ rejoices with the truth.

_____ always protects.

_____ always trusts.

_____ always hopes.

_____ always perseveres.

_____ never fails.

1a. Next, try *your name* in each blank. You might squirm with some of them (we did), but realize that the Holy Spirit is building up these love traits inside of you. As Christians, we are changing daily as we become more Christ-like.

2. Take a moment and consider your life. Where do you think the Holy Spirit has brought the greatest change in you when it comes to these love traits? Where have you grown the most?

3. Pick three of the love traits from Question #1 that you want **to be strengthened** in your life.

     1._____

     2._____

     3._____

Take a moment to pray, asking for the Lord's empowerment to grow in love in these three areas.

4. Try your kid's name in each blank. Which of these traits do your children best show love?

5. Pick three of these love traits that you want to encourage your child to develop in their life. (The top 3 may differ with each child.)

1.	1.	1.
2.	2.	2.
3.	3.	3.

Once again, take some time to pray, asking God how you can help your kids become more loving in these ways.

Embraced by Jesus

Life Before Meeting Jesus

Eric: I grew up without much religion. My family never went to any church or religious event. My mom did teach me to pray before dinner and at bedtime, but those were memorized prayers in her native language of German that I didn't fully understand. Praying was more of a cultural habit than anything genuine on my part.

I had no idea who Jesus was, except that some bumper stickers claimed he was a lord.

One day in high school, my English teacher gave the class an interest survey to fill out. It was meant to help us in our future career choices because it highlighted our areas of interest and disinterest. I don't remember what that survey showed to be my greatest interests but I do remember that there was one area where I ranked the lowest in the whole class: the area of religion. That was me- heathen Eric.

Sin Denial

Although God has done great things for every human who has ever existed, many refuse to acknowledge him or his deeds. Too many of us are blind to what he is doing around us. Too many of us are ignorant. We go through life without ever asking the tough questions about why we exist and why we do wrong things that hurt us and others. We sin and don't want to admit it, nor do we want to admit that there is a God who can hold us accountable for our actions.

The Holy Spirit at Work

However, the Holy Spirit is always at work in people's lives. He is convicting of sin and wooing people toward our Heavenly Father. Jesus said it this way:

> "But very truly I tell you, it is for your good that I am going away. Unless I go away, the Advocate will not come to you; but if I go, I will send him to you. When he comes, he will prove the world to be in the wrong

about sin and righteousness and judgment: about sin, because people do not believe in me; about righteousness, because I am going to the Father, where you can see me no longer; and about judgment, because the prince of this world now stands condemned." (John 16:7-11 NIV)

The Holy Spirit shows us our need for salvation. God reveals the truth to our heart, that he loves us dearly and sent his Son to die on the cross for our wrongs:

"For God so loved the world that he gave his one and only Son, that whoever believes in him shall not perish but have eternal life. For God did not send his Son into the world to condemn the world, but to save the world through him. Whoever believes in him is not condemned, but whoever does not believe stands condemned already because they have not believed in the name of God's one and only Son." (John 3:16-18 NIV)

Eric: I was a heathen, but the Holy Spirit was still working. Within two years of that high school interest survey, I became a new person in Christ. Maybe it was that awful score in religion that motivated me, but I became curious about religious things. I read books about the end-times. I read through a Bible that one of my sisters had left behind when she moved out. I started regularly watching a TV preacher on Sunday mornings. And then one day while I was reading in Psalm 22, I remembered what that preacher had said about Jesus' sacrifice for me on the cross and it all made sense.

I cried.

I changed.

Jesus embraced me and all I could do was thank him for my salvation.

I responded to what Jesus had done for me on the cross. He had embraced me in his love and I hugged him back.

That Fall day during my senior year in high school, I became a Christ follower.

Salvation Changes Everything

In everyone's life, there comes a time for a decision, a moment when we either choose to accept Jesus' offer of salvation or refuse it. We either embrace him or reject him. Accepting his offer starts a whole new life for us, whether it happens as a young child (like it did for Amy), or as an 18-year-old teen (like it did for Eric), or when we are in the very last years of a long life (as it did for Eric's dad).

Entering into salvation changes us, and the Holy Spirit continues that changing from that day onward. We realize his sacrificial love for us and we love him in return. That love from us ought to be more than just a feeling; it is meant to be a love in action, a love so strong that it drives our life decisions and our moral choices.

That is true for us and for our children.

Daily Response

1. Do you remember the first time you realized that Jesus loved you? What was that like?

2. Are you thankful for your salvation? If so, take a moment to write down what your salvation means to you. How has your salvation changed you?

3a. Do your children know your salvation story? If not please share it with them, because your salvation is part of their family history.

3b. Do your children know that Jesus loves them and chose to die for their sins? Have your children confessed that Jesus is Lord and believed in their heart that God raised him from the dead? (Romans 10:9)

If Yes, take some time this week to remind them of that and give thanks to Jesus for his sacrificial love.

If No, please take some time this week to share this life-giving truth with them. As a parent, there is nothing greater you can do than leading your child to God.

Embracing Jesus in Return

Trusting God isn't Easy

Amy: Some things in life are not optional. I have to do certain things, whether I understand every "why" or "how." Scriptures tell us to love God, but that isn't always easy, because sometimes I don't understand his reasons for denying good things from happening. I've prayed for healings, salvations, job advancements, and direction in life, but they didn't occur. That's hard, because all of them seemed like good requests, like things God should care about too. But then nothing…

In college, I applied to become a Resident Advisor for one of the women's dorms. It seemed like the perfect position, allowing me to mentor incoming freshmen while also getting free housing and food. I took a required training class and did well. I prayed hard and was very hopeful I would get the position, but then I got really sick on the day of the interview. I missed my opportunity and I never became an RA. My prayers and preparation seemed for nothing…

Currently, I'm praying for a teaching job closer to home so that I can be more involved in my community and spend more time with my family. Eric and I want to start a ministry to our trio of towns, but God hasn't opened that door yet. I want to cut my 30-mile commute, so I've diligently applied for openings and done numerous interviews, but no new job. It might still happen, but so far nothing…

I've seen my boys pray for silly things like a snow day and for serious things like a sick loved one, but God's response wasn't always "yes". It is hard to explain God's love to them when they are mourning the death of their beloved cat or the breaking up of a friendship. I try to give them answers, but sometimes I have nothing…

Unanswered Prayer

My grandmother spent most of her life praying for her prodigal youngest son, but died before ever seeing any results to her prayers. It wasn't until many years later that Uncle Steve finally repented of his horrible life of abuse and debauchery. In the last few years of his life, he often sat in the back pew of a small church, crying profusely as he repented of so much.

He changed, yet his mother never got to see that, at least not during her life.

In reality, we might never see an answer to some of our prayers. How many times have we prayed for situations and never seen the answer we longed to experience? And yet we are told to still love him. How do we do that?

Hug Jesus

We don't have all the answers, but we should still step forward and hug our Lord. We may be confused or angry or feeling hurt, but we should still embrace him even without having all of our questions answered or all of our problems solved. If we trust him with our soul, then we need to trust him with everything else too.

Embrace Jesus, even when you don't understand everything around you. If you need to, cry into his shoulder or even yell into his ear, but still hug him.

Love God Completely

As Christians, we are called to embrace the Lord who has saved us:

> Jesus replied: " 'Love the Lord your God with all your heart and with all your soul and with all your mind.' This is the first and greatest commandment. And the second is like it: 'Love your neighbor as yourself.' All the Law and the Prophets hang on these two commandments." (Matthew 22:37-40 NIV)

We are to love God with all of our heart, soul, and mind. That is not something *done* in a split-second decision to accept Christ's offer of salvation. It is something that *begins* at salvation but it *continues* throughout our life and on into eternity.

We are called to a life of love.

So what does it mean to love "with all your heat and with all soul and with all your mind"? It means putting everything into it: your emotions, desires, intellect, affections, and energy. We are to love God without reservation. We are to love him with our whole being, not holding back. How can we not love him with total abandonment, after he's done so much for us?

> "This is how God showed his love among us: He sent his one and only Son into the world that we might live through him. This is love: not that we loved God, but that he loved us and sent his Son as an atoning sacrifice for our sins." (1 John 4:9-10 NIV)

"We love because he first loved us." (1 John 4:19 NIV)

Love Reciprocated

We want to see the fruit of the Spirit in our lives and in the lives of our children, and part of that fruit is love. This is a love for the God who made us, saved us, and sustains us through every day. His sacrificial love for us should spur us to love him all the more. Jesus is our role model. He shows us how to love him and how to love others.

Daily Response

1. How do you show Jesus that you love him?

2. What are some life decisions that you've made that were affected by your love of God?

3. How can you **model** to your children how to love Jesus? How can you show them how to *hug God?*

4. How can you **teach** your children to love Jesus? How can you instruct them on having a relationship with God?

Loving our Kids

Love Expressed

Eric: "I love hugs!" That has become a regular declaration in our household, starting a few years ago. It wasn't that we didn't love hugs before then, but I realized it was something our family needed to be more proactive about. Our younger son would usually come get a hug whenever he needed one, but I started noticing that our older one was holding back. Maybe it was his more reserved personality. Maybe it was the fact that he was now a "big middle schooler" and almost a teenager. Whatever the reasons, I sensed that he wanted more physical touch yet was unsure how to engage. Realizing that, I knew I had to change something.

I decided that I needed to get things started with my son. I would say something like, "Can I have hug? I would really enjoy one of your hugs right now." He would do so, at first almost hesitantly, but soon his inhibitions evaporated. These days, he's often the one starting the hugs with me, with Amy, with his brother, or even with other relatives and close friends.

Physical affection may not be a problem in your family, but I wasn't raised in your typical American home. I'm the youngest of six and only the last two of us were born here in the USA. We were an immigrant household: eating ethnic foods, speaking a different language, and participating in family customs that were flavored by my parents' homeland. They were from Hamburg, so they taught us the reserved culture of northern Europe: a stoic, emotions-in-check kind of lifestyle. In our home, hugs were infrequent and kisses were reserved to small pecks between Mutti and Vati when they were in front of us. Praise was given as earned. Words of affection were rare. My parents loved me, but they showed it in more subtle ways.

Even though I was determined to raise my kids with more overt attention and affection, that stoicism still slipped in. I didn't mean to, but I wasn't showing love to my oldest son in a way that he needed.

Separation

Sometimes there can be a disconnect between us and our children. It usually doesn't happen on purpose; it just slips in. A wall starts to grow between us and our kid, and unfortunately that wall can get taller and wider and thicker with the passing of each year. If we don't change things, we could end up completely alienated from our child. What might start as difference in personality or temperament or interests, can develop into distancing, exasperation, or even anger. Why aren't they more like me? Why do they have to be so difficult? Don't they realize that I love them?

Parental Love

The Apostle Paul was a spiritual father to the church he started in the city of Thessalonica. As the years passed, not everyone there appreciated his spiritual parenting. Some grew distant toward Paul, causing him to defend himself in one of his letters. He sought to clarify his motives and his feelings.

Read 1 Thessalonians, chapter 2

Paul uses a lot of parent-child word pictures in this chapter. He and his companions came to that city with the innocence of young children (v. 7), having no hidden motives. Paul and his companions were as nurturing as a nursing mother, caring that deeply for this new-born church.

Finally, Paul says that they acted like a father toward this group of believers, doing three things that all of us should do with our kids:

> For you know that we dealt with each of you as a father deals with his
> own children, encouraging, comforting and urging you to live lives worthy
> of God, who calls you into his kingdom and glory.
> (1 Thessalonians 2:11-12 NIV)

Three Ways to Show Love

We love our kids but we might not understand them completely, just like Paul didn't fully understand why some in Thessalonica were distancing from him. We might not understand, but we still need to do these three things mentioned in the verses above:

1. Encourage
2. Comfort
3. Urge them to live lives worthy of God

What a great list for how to show love to our children. We might not share the same interests with our child (sports, arts, hobbies, academics) but we can still cheer them on. We might not fully understand why that missed goal was so important to them, but we can still offer a shoulder to cry on. We might not understand their choice of careers or life-goals, but we still need to urge them to pursue it in a way that honors God.

Daily Response

1. Share at least three ways you show your love to your kids:

2. How do you think you could do better at showing love towards them?

3. How do your kids show their love to you?

Loving Others

Playground Pest

Eric: Our son labeled this particular boy as his foe, because even third graders can have mortal enemies. What awful things had the other boy done? Well, the kid was obnoxious and assertive, outgoing where our son was an introvert, a risk-taker where our son was someone who loved to be cautious. This boy's greatest crime, however, was that he was being a pest to the girls in their 3rd grade class. Our bashful son's few friends were mainly female, so he couldn't stand that this boy was pestering them. Our son even plotted ways to avenge the teasing of his buddies. He certainly had no desire to ever socialize with this other kid, even though Amy and I liked his parents and really thought our son could use a more-outgoing friend. Nope, that was not going to happen. Not from our son. There were no feelings of love for this other kid- he was the enemy to be attacked and neutralized, although our son wasn't one to really resort to physical violence.

Label and Discard

Sometimes, we are prone to label people as "enemy" and then feel justified to never show any love toward them. Why should we show them any love? They don't deserve it. Once we have labeled them as "enemy" we can discard them from our life. We avoid them or give them a cold-shoulder. We talk behind their back and warn others to avoid them. We do our best to isolate them away from us. Sometimes we plot revenge, maybe calling it "teaching them a lesson." And we usually feel justified in all of this.

One of my (Eric) pet peeves are the parents who rudely drive around the drop-off lane at school to cut to the front, where they let out their little darlings and then wait in their car (that's now blocking everyone else), just to watch Junior and Precious slowly meander up to the buildings. Aargh! One of the guilty ones is the co-owner of a local restaurant and I'll admit telling Amy more than once that I don't want to eat at her restaurant anymore. She's probably in a hurry to get back for the breakfast rush, but I have no pity on her. After all, she cut to the front of the line and delayed my own kid-drop by two or three minutes! The nerve!

We can be quick to label someone as an enemy. An acquaintance seems to ignore us at a gathering. A stranger cuts us off on the interstate. Someone sneaks to front of the line at the coffeehouse. Another parent seems to slight our child. We see or experience something unpleasant and instantly assume the other person did it on purpose and with bad motives. We see it as a declaration of war and we will get our revenge!

However, Jesus has other intentions for us. He wants us known for our love, not for our hate.

Loving Enemies

Jesus said a lot of things that are hard to obey. We can be tempted to skip those verses because his words make us uncomfortable as we realize how far we are from his directions. Words like these:

> "'But to you who are listening I say: Love your enemies, do good to those who hate you, bless those who curse you, pray for those who mistreat you. If someone slaps you on one cheek, turn to them the other also. If someone takes your coat, do not withhold your shirt from them. Give to everyone who asks you, and if anyone takes what belongs to you, do not demand it back. Do to others as you would have them do to you.
>
> 'If you love those who love you, what credit is that to you? Even sinners love those who love them. And if you do good to those who are good to you, what credit is that to you? Even sinners do that. And if you lend to those from whom you expect repayment, what credit is that to you? Even sinners lend to sinners, expecting to be repaid in full. But love your enemies, do good to them, and lend to them without expecting to get anything back. Then your reward will be great, and you will be children of the Most High, because he is kind to the ungrateful and wicked. Be merciful, just as your Father is merciful.'" (Luke 6:27-36 NIV)

Obeying Jesus

Amy and I don't know how these words from Jesus hit you, but for us this is hard to hear. All of us want to love people who we think deserve our love. But there are people in our lives who we would rather ignore or avoid or even punish for what they have done to us or others who we care about. We don't want to love those particular *others*.

One of the reasons it is hard to comprehend loving a stranger or an enemy is that we forget what love looks like. We aren't being told to give them roses or go out on a romantic date with a bad person. Instead, Jesus is asking us to do practical acts of love: do good, pray, offer a second chance, give, lend, forgive. He isn't asking us to join them in their sins. He isn't asking us to let them keep abusing us. He isn't asking us to let them move into our home.

What Jesus is telling us to do is to show love towards everyone, even those we might think undeserving of it. That love is practical, it is doing good toward the other person, rather than being bad toward them. We didn't deserve Jesus' act of sacrificial love, but he still loved us so much that he died for us. Now, he wants us to show God's love toward others, even those we don't like... even those we don't feel deserving of our love.

Our son, who is now well past third grade, never did act out the worst of his revenge plots and, eventually, became friends with that other kid. As for Eric and that mom who likes to cut to the front of the drop-off line... well, he realizes it's about time for him to visit her restaurant again and maybe look for a chance to minister to her and her husband.

Daily Response

1. The words of Jesus are sometimes hard to hear. His orders make us squirm because what he's asking us to do is so counter-intuitive, so foreign to what society would tell us to do.

Pick the top 3 hardest ones for you:

1. ___ Doing good for someone who hates you.
2. ___ Blessing someone who curses you.
3. ___ Praying for someone who mistreats you.
4. ___ Turning the other cheek when slapped.
5. ___ Surrendering your shirt to someone who has already taken your coat.
6. ___ Giving to everyone who asks.
7. ___ Not demanding the returning of your stuff after someone has taken it.
8. ___ Doing to others as you would have them do to you.

2. Why do you think Jesus would ask us to show love in this way? How is this a reflection of God's love for us?

3. How can you *model* "loving others" to your children?

4. How can you *teach* your children to love others better?

Gathering ending Week 1
Notes

The Fruit of

Joy

But the fruit of the Spirit is love, **joy**, peace, forbearance, kindness, goodness, faithfulness, gentleness and self-control. Against such things there is no law. (Galatians 5:22-23 NIV *emphasis added*)

What is Joy?

Is Your Soul Satisfied?

Eric: Have you ever experienced joy and sadness mixed? I have. When my mother died three months after a major stroke, I felt a weird combination of the two. I rejoiced that she was free from the pain and frailty. I wept at the loss of her sweet encouragement and her soft smile. I rejoiced that she was in our Lord's presence and was now reunited with many loved ones who had already passed, including my father (who had died a decade earlier). But I also hurt from that gap in my life that my Mutti so abundantly filled.

Even now, as I write this, I'm smiling even as my eyes fill up. I'm not happy, but I'm joyful in the middle of a remembered loss.

For me, joy is different from happiness. Joy is deeper and can be there even during tough times, while *being happy* is a temporary emotional state. I enjoy being happy, but that happiness fades away after a few days… hours… minutes…

Joy is so much greater than just "being happy". Joy can last a lifetime, because **joy is soul satisfaction**. As we learn to trust God, he fills us with joy and peace.

God doesn't ask me to be happy all the time, but he does tell me to rejoice always, and I don't think he would ask something that's impossible.

Choosing Joy

If we are honest, most of us would admit to having a hard time grasping that *joy* is a choice. Because we often confuse joy with fleeting happiness, we think it's just something that happens to us. We see joy as something that we can't control. If the situation or circumstances are perfect, then joy might appear like the sun peeking through the clouds after a rainy day. We act as if joy comes and goes, arriving at unexpected moments and leaving far too quickly.

However, the Bible paints a different picture of joy. Joy is shown to be an integral part of the fruit of the Spirit. Joy is vital in walking by the Spirit, for us and for our children, so we need to get a good understanding of what it means to have joy and to rejoice.

Letter of Joy

Paul, in jail for being an outspoken Christian, writes a letter to a group of believers whom he dearly loves that are also going through hard times. Most of us wouldn't be bubbling over with joy if we were locked up, but Paul is. Most of us wouldn't dare to talk about joy with folks who are struggling themselves, but Paul does. His letter to the Christians in the city of Philippi mentions "joy" or "rejoice" over a dozen times. Some have called this the *Letter of Joy* because he uses the term so often, and yet he wrote this while being unjustly incarcerated and wrote it to people who were themselves being persecuted for their faith.

He starts the letter by sharing that his prayers for them were always full of joy:

> "I thank my God every time I remember you. In all my prayers for all of you, I always pray with joy because of your partnership in the gospel from the first day until now, being confident of this, that he who began a good work in you will carry it on to completion until the day of Christ Jesus." (Philippians 1:3-6 NIV)

Joy List

Paul shares so many things that he's joyful about or wants them to be joyful about in this letter:

1. **Paul** prays for **them** with joy. (1:4)
2. **Paul** has joy in the good results of Jesus being preached, even when some did this for the wrong reasons. (1:18)
3. **Paul** has joy in being prayed for by **them**. (1:18-19)
4. **Paul** has joy for the provision of the Holy Spirit. (1:18-19)
5. **Paul** appreciates and has a part in **their** progress and joy in the faith. (1:25)
6. **Paul** has joy in anticipation of good changes in **them**. (2:2)
7. **Paul** has joy in **their** hard work and commitment. (2:17)
8. **Paul** asks **them** to join him in his joy. (2:18)
9. **Paul** knows that **they** will rejoice over another's recovery from almost dying. (2:28)
10. **Paul** asks **them** to welcome with great joy those who risk their lives in service to others. (2:29)
11. **Paul** tells **them** to rejoice in the Lord (3:1)
12. **Paul** declares that **they** are his joy and crown (4:1)
13. **Paul** tells **them** to rejoice in the Lord always. (4:4)
14. **Paul** tells **them** again, rejoice in the Lord. (4:4)
15. **Paul** rejoices in the Lord that **they** have helped him. (4:10)

Paul is well aware that joy is different from *being happy*. He is encouraging us to embrace joy even during difficulties. As a matter of fact, right after he tells them to rejoice in the Lord always, he acknowledges that they face anxiety and real needs too.

> "Do not be anxious about anything, but in every situation, by prayer and petition, with thanksgiving, present your requests to God. And the peace of God, which transcends all understanding, will guard your hearts and your minds in Christ Jesus." (Philippians 4:6-7 NIV)

Paul also acknowledges that sometimes we need to take a moment to find a better focus in our lives. It is hard to rejoice when we are only looking at bad things. Instead, he encourages us to refocus, concentrating on better things:

> "Finally, brothers and sisters, whatever is true, whatever is noble, whatever is right, whatever is pure, whatever is lovely, whatever is admirable—if anything is excellent or praiseworthy—think about such things. Whatever you have learned or received or heard from me, or seen in me—put it into practice. And the God of peace will be with you." (Philippians 4:8-9 NIV)

Choose Joy

The opposite of joy isn't sorrow or misery or even anxiety. As shared at the beginning of today's entry, you can have joy and sadness at the same time. No, **the opposite of joy is a deadening selfishness**. Where joy looks outward and especially upward to God, the opposite of joy looks inward at self and dissatisfaction in yourself or your situation.

Life is rarely as perfect as we want it to be, but we have a choice on how we react to our imperfect, sometimes-hard, sometimes-disappointing life. Will we choose joy or choose to be joyless?

Joy in the good.

Joy in spite of the bad.

Joy even during the mediocre, grinding busyness of everyday life.

We all need joy, so isn't it wonderful that we can actually make the choice to rejoice?

Daily Response

1. Sometimes it can seem hard to find anything to rejoice in, but it's worthwhile to make the effort. Take a moment to review the Joy List mentioned earlier and try a quick word replacement in those 15 statements.

Put in **your name** for Paul's.

Put in your **childs' names** for their/them.

2. Which of those 15 statements stand out to you the most once you insert yourself and your kids? Why?

3. How can you teach your children to be joyful in life, even when things aren't going perfect? What should they be joyful about?

Rejoicing in the Good

Fighting for What's Right

Eric: My kids have great imaginations, pretending to be all sorts of characters and having so many different adventures. They have been warriors and dinosaurs, inventors and explorers. I've seen boxes turn into cars, and couches become spaceships. I've even helped turn a dining table set and a pile of pillows into an impenetrable fortress. (That transformation happened just in time, because I suddenly turned into a roaring monster but was unable to break into their safe haven.)

In all those make-believe struggles, my kids were battling for the good. They conquered armies, rescued friends in danger, thwarted space invasions, stopped marauding dinosaur packs, and recovered lost treasures. Each victory brings them joy, a satisfaction that an imaginary injustice has been prevented. When their play is done, the villain is defeated, wrongs are righted, and the world is safe again.

My kids are usually the hero of their own story, because that is what they want to be in real life. They want to make a difference and stand up for what is right. I was the same way as a kid, weren't you?

Joy in Justice

As parents, we want to teach our kids to celebrate the good. We want them to rejoice and embrace the right and reject the wrong. We don't just want to teach them right-from-wrong, but we want them live it out for all their lives, to find joy in the good. It is just like what the writer of Proverbs said, "When justice is done, it brings joy to the righteous but terror to evildoers." (Proverbs 21:15 NIV)

Unfortunately, we live in a world that often isn't fair or just. Evil gets celebrated. Good gets mocked or knocked down. So how can we teach our kids to rejoice in the good when society around them is doing the opposite? How do we get them to find joy in justice without growing hardened by an unfair world?

The Hero Wins

Sometimes we need to be reminded that we are ambassadors for another country: the Kingdom of Heaven. It is fine to have pride in our earthly country, but our first loyalty is to our God and his kingdom. In Revelations we get a vision of what is ahead for us, a place without pain or mourning, a place where our true hero is in charge and has made everything right. In Revelation, Jesus is pictured as a warrior riding from heaven to victory over the earth:

> I saw heaven standing open and there before me was a white horse, whose rider is called Faithful and True. With justice he judges and wages war. His eyes are like blazing fire, and on his head are many crowns. He has a name written on him that no one knows but he himself. He is dressed in a robe dipped in blood, and his name is the Word of God. The armies of heaven were following him, riding on white horses and dressed in fine linen, white and clean. Coming out of his mouth is a sharp sword with which to strike down the nations. "He will rule them with an iron scepter." He treads the winepress of the fury of the wrath of God Almighty. On his robe and on his thigh he has this name written: king of kings and lord of lords. (Revelation 19:11-16 NIV)

A bit later in the book we read of his final righting of all wrongs, ending death, suffering, and tears:

> Then I saw "a new heaven and a new earth," for the first heaven and the first earth had passed away, and there was no longer any sea. I saw the Holy City, the new Jerusalem, coming down out of heaven from God, prepared as a bride beautifully dressed for her husband. And I heard a loud voice from the throne saying, "Look! God's dwelling place is now among the people, and he will dwell with them. They will be his people, and God himself will be with them and be their God. 'He will wipe every tear from their eyes. There will be no more death' or mourning or crying or pain, for the old order of things has passed away." (Revelation 21:1-4 NIV)

So we have that *good* to look forward to up ahead and that is good, because sometime it seems like a fight to get there. Like in all good heroic tales, it seems that in our life we need to face that battle, that resistance, that struggle to win through. The author of Hebrews shares in chapter 11 what some call the "Hall of Faith"- a list of the spiritual heroes who went ahead of us. Then in chapter 12 the author shares this:

> Therefore, since we are surrounded by such a great cloud of witnesses, let us throw off everything that hinders and the sin that so easily entangles. And let us run with perseverance the race marked out for us, fixing our eyes on Jesus, the pioneer and perfecter of faith. **For the joy set before him** he endured the cross, scorning its shame, and sat down at the right hand of the throne of God. Consider him who endured such opposition from sinners, so that you will not grow weary and lose heart. (Hebrews 12:1-3 NIV, emphasis added)

Jesus has done so much for us and he did so knowing that it would result in the joy of us being reconciled with him.

There is joy found in Jesus' goodness.

There is encouragement there too, helping us to run our own lifelong race.

The Ultimate Good

There is joy to be found in focusing on the good. Where the world around us often wants to bad-mouth or even celebrate the villain, we are called to keep our eyes on Jesus instead- the ultimate Good Guy. Our children need to learn to rejoice in the good too.

We aren't talking about trying to turn Jesus into a cheesy cartoon superhero (he doesn't look right in a cape anyway). But we are talking about making sure our kids know what a real hero looks like, someone who set aside his divinity to take on a human form and lived among us. Someone who sacrificed himself for all of humanity. Do our kids really know Jesus and the good he did? Have we modeled to them what it means to rejoice over such good?

Daily Response

1. What good can you rejoice in today? List all the good you can think of.

2. Does your child know the good that Jesus has done? What more can you teach them?

3. How can you model "rejoicing in the good" to your children?

Joy in Celebrating our Kids

Goal!!!!

Amy: Back in 2021 during the COVID pandemic, one of our boys was struggling with distance learning and hungered for friends. We decided to put him in the sport of his choice to hopefully build up his confidence and restore some community in his life. He chose soccer, which he had never played before. That spring his skill gap wasn't so obvious because all the kids were out-of-practice, but when he returned for the fall season, his inexperience was glaringly obvious. It was hard to hear my son question why he was even playing when the others were so much better at the sport.

There were no goals to celebrate. He didn't come in first place at practice runs. He struggled to keep up with competitors who were far more seasoned. He questioned himself at times, but he didn't quit. He practiced, tried his best, and slowly improved. But he still didn't score any points.

We brought him to his twice-weekly practices and came as a family to every game, but the most he became that first year was a mediocre player. How do you celebrate your kids when they aren't great at something? What is there to cheer and shout about?

For Eric, the additional challenge was that he comes from a family that isn't demonstrative. When he was a kid, no one was yelling from the stands or shouting encouragement in the auditorium. It's hard for him to be a loud cheerleader for anyone, because he prefers to be stoic. He and I aren't the boisterous kind.

Not my Place to Celebrate

Celebrating our kids in public isn't always easy. Maybe you aren't the kind of person who gets loud. Maybe you have a hard time finding anything worth celebrating.

Sometimes we are too busy to even notice the milestones in their life, failing to celebrate their huge steps, like:

- First time walking, talking, eating solid food
- Learning to ride a bike, shoot a basket, roller skate, color in the lines, etc.
- First day of preschool, elementary, middle school, high school, trade school, college
- Graduating preschool, elementary, middle school, high school, trade school, college

- Getting their first Bible
- Sport Victories
- School Awards
- Entering Puberty
- Earning a Driver's License
- Coming to Salvation, Baptism
- First Date
- First Job
- Getting Engaged, Married, and Having their own Children

There are so many events that we could celebrate, but sometimes we don't know how. Maybe no one celebrated over us. Maybe our "kid" isn't our actual biological offspring and so we feel a bit out-of-place doing the partying on their behalf- we think that some other person should be doing the celebrating over them. Well, let's see what the Bible shows us about that.

Celebrate in Biblical Proportions

Not all of "our kids" are necessarily our biological offspring. The Apostle John felt like a spiritual father to the believers that he had mentored and he was gladdened when others spoke of their spiritual strength:

> I have no greater joy than to hear that my children are walking in the truth. (3 John 1:4 NIV)

The Apostle Paul mentored numerous young men in the faith, like Timothy, Silas, and Titus. He too celebrated their accomplishments and urged them on in their spiritual growth as young men:

> These, then, are the things you should teach. Encourage and rebuke with all authority. Do not let anyone despise you. (Titus 2:15 NIV)

> Recalling your tears, I long to see you, so that I may be filled with joy. (2 Timothy 1:4 NIV)

We need to encourage and exhort all the children who look to us as a parent or mentor, because they need us. Our joy over them will uplift and infuse them with greater courage to go on with life.

Follow God's Example

Celebrating our kids is Biblical. We should publicly praise and cheer on our children. Our heavenly Father set that example for us many times. At the time of his Son's birth, he sent his angels to announce and celebrate the event:

> And there were shepherds living out in the fields nearby, keeping watch over their flocks at night. An angel of the Lord appeared to them, and the glory of the Lord shone around them, and they were terrified. But the angel said to them, "Do not be afraid. I bring you good news that will cause great joy for all the people. Today in the town of David a Savior has been born to you; he is the Messiah, the Lord." (Luke 2:8-11 NIV)

God himself shows us how we should celebrate our children. When his Son was baptized, the Father spoke out for all to hear, announcing his love for Jesus and how pleased he was with him:

> As soon as Jesus was baptized, he went up out of the water. At that moment heaven was opened, and he saw the Spirit of God descending like a dove and alighting on him. And a voice from heaven said, "This is my Son, whom I love; with him I am well pleased."
> (Matthew 3:16-17 NIV)

Public Praise

The example Father God gives us is to be open and public in our praise. He celebrated important moments in Jesus' life (like birth and baptism), and told others how much he loved his Son. The Father was quite open about the fact that he was pleased with Jesus.

With our soccer playing son, we learned to celebrate every small victory, like taking the ball from an opponent or successfully passing to a team member. Even though our son was a mediocre player that first year, he landed on a great team under a fantastic coach who kept encouraging and pushing all of them. His team beat all the others to become the citywide champs for that age group, and then they went on to become the regional champs too. He was so excited! Our so-so player ended up with a trophy and two medals. That second medal he received came from his coach, who declared him the team's most-improved player.

Since it was his first year, he obviously wasn't the best player on the team. However, soccer is a team sport, so every team member earned a trophy. They did this together, even if some had greater skill or natural abilities than others. And we celebrated all of it with him.

God gives us the example to celebrate with our children. We should announce in front of others how pleased we are with our kids and how much we love them. We should definitely celebrate those key moments in their life.

Daily Response

1. Think back to the last time you celebrated your kid's life. What was the occasion? What did you do to celebrate?

2. Every birthday we hang streamers over our dining room table, setting up a candle-topped cake and at least a few presents; you will be forgiven if the gift count is low or if you forget the ice cream, but it's not a birthday celebration in our home without streamers. What are some of your family's unique celebration rituals?

3. How are you teaching your kids to celebrate? What more could you do to model celebrating to them?

Joy- No Matter What

Smile for the Camera!

Eric: "Smile." If you are like most other humans in this world, you've gotten that order hundreds of times in your life. As a kid, you had to smile almost every time your photo was being taken. You were taught that smiling is the polite thing to do. You were probably told to smile when meeting someone for the first time or when going for a job interview or making a speech or accepting a present from grandma. Smile, even if you don't really feel like smiling.

If necessary, fake the happiness.

In Philippians we are told to "Rejoice in the Lord always. I will say it again: Rejoice!" (Philippians 4:4 NIV). How is this different from the time your teacher ordered everyone to "smile" because she didn't want the class photo ruined by a sour face? Is the Bible asking us to fake happiness? I don't think so.

Like many of you, I've experienced the death of loved ones, disappointments in life, failures, sick children, injuries, injustices, and struggles. Sometimes, life punches you in the gut and leaves you gasping for air. Why is that? How can I respond to the awful times with joy?

I've experienced these two truths that seem to be contradictory:

Truth #1- Life is really hard and unfair at times.

Truth #2- God is good.

How can we reconcile the two?

Choosing Joy

When it says, "Rejoice in the Lord always. I will say it again: Rejoice!" you'll notice that we are being told to have joy. The Bible implies that we can choose to rejoice or not. That is a hard truth to grasp. Unless it has happened to you before, it is hard to imagine having joy in the midst of pain or disappointment or loss. Whereas *happiness* just happens, the Bible states that we can make the conscious decision to go the way of joy.

No matter our circumstances.

This isn't a giddy feeling that we have to conjure up, in complete denial of reality. We've met those kind of chipper chaps before, folks who claim "all is well" even while life is crumbling around them. No, the Lord is not calling us into a fantasy life where we pretend everything is smiles and sunshine.

This isn't a "finding pleasure in the pain" message either. We aren't called to be glad about the heartache or agony; we aren't meant to be sadomasochists who love suffering. Instead, we are invited to find joy even while the bad is happening in our life.

Finally, this isn't something new to our generation. Christians for centuries have embraced joy while facing tough times. Some of them faced some really tough circumstances. For many of them, it helped when they realized they weren't the only ones going through this and that their troubles could produce a witness for Jesus and even good changes in their own lives.

Joy in the Midst of It

James, the brother of Jesus, encourages us to consider it pure joy that the bad experiences can mature us as believers:

> Consider it **pure joy**, my brothers and sisters, whenever you face trials
> of many kinds, because you know that the testing of your faith produces
> perseverance. Let perseverance finish its work so that you may be mature
> and complete, not lacking anything.
> (James 1:2-4 NIV- emphasis added)

Peter, who was there in the midst of Jesus' earthly ministry and watched him go up on that cross, wants us to rejoice even when we suffer as Christians. We can find joy because we know the ultimate outcome will be the inheritance that is safeguarded for us:

> Praise be to the God and Father of our Lord Jesus Christ! In his great
> mercy he has given us new birth into a living hope through the resurrection
> of Jesus Christ from the dead, and into an inheritance that can never perish,
> spoil or fade. This inheritance is kept in heaven for you, who through faith
> are shielded by God's power until the coming of the salvation that is ready
> to be revealed in the last time. In all this you greatly **rejoice**, though now
> for a little while you may have had to suffer grief in all kinds of trials. These
> have come so that the proven genuineness of your faith—of greater worth
> than gold, which perishes even though refined by fire—may result in
> praise, glory and honor when Jesus Christ is revealed. Though you have

not seen him, you love him; and even though you do not see him now, you believe in him and are filled with an inexpressible and glorious **joy**, for you are receiving the end result of your faith, the salvation of your souls. (1 Peter 1:3-9 NIV- emphasis added)

Dear friends, do not be surprised at the fiery ordeal that has come on you to test you, as though something strange were happening to you. But **rejoice** inasmuch as you participate in the sufferings of Christ, so that you may be **overjoyed** when his glory is revealed. If you are insulted because of the name of Christ, you are blessed, for the Spirit of glory and of God rests on you. If you suffer, it should not be as a murderer or thief or any other kind of criminal, or even as a meddler. However, if you suffer as a Christian, do not be ashamed, but praise God that you bear that name. (1 Peter 4:13-16 NIV- emphasis added)

The Psalmist recognized how God can change our lives so completely:

You turned my wailing into dancing; you removed my sackcloth and clothed me with **joy**, that my heart may sing your praises and not be silent. Lord my God, I will praise you forever. (Psalm 30:11-12 NIV- emphasis added)

Soul Satisfaction

Many of us have cried in heartache and still smiled at knowing his comforting embrace. Life can really suck, but Jesus has still saved us and his Holy Spirit is with us as a promise of redemption in the end. As bad as it can get, we can still look forward to being with him for all eternity. We can still "rejoice in the Lord," in who he is and what he has done, even while suffering through terrible times. Some have called this *soul satisfaction,* which is a good way to look at it. The Joy we are asked to have is one that comes from our soul being at peace even when our world is in turmoil. We might not understand how the two truths mentioned above are reconciled, but somehow they can both exist at the same time: 1) life gets hard, and 2) God is always good.

Choosing joy isn't always easy, but it's worth it. Three obstacles come to mind that might keep us from joy:

1. We are concentrated on the bad only.
2. We don't see how this bad could ever be helpful for anyone, especially not for us.
3. We forget that we serve a bigger cause- that we are ambassadors of God's kingdom.

Daily Response

1. Have you ever faced a time when you found joy in the midst of hard times?

2. What are some of the difficulties your kid(s) face today?

3. How can you help your kid(s) embrace joy no matter what?

Living a Joyful Life

Fear of the Future

Eric: What do you do with an eight-year-old who's worried about growing old? I faced that as I was tucking one of my kids into bed a few years ago. Earlier that day, my son had gone grocery shopping with Amy and they had passed the shelves of "adult diapers". He asked questions and Amy explained their purpose then they continued shopping without any further questions or comments. But, apparently, he mused about it for the rest of the day.

By bedtime, he couldn't fall asleep because he was worried that some day he would have to wear diapers again.

My eight-year-old was worrying about becoming eighty.

Careful not to chuckle, I had to assure him the day for adult diapers was far, far away for him, and that it might never happen.

It might seem silly to me to worry about senior incontinence when you are only 8, but I have my own share of future fears that are just as silly. Fearing failure or rejection, I often held back. I hesitated to try new things. Sometimes, I've analyzed and debated taking a risk that I missed the window of opportunity. I did it in my dating life, in my career, and in friendships. Worry about future failure or rejection, kept me from doing what I could now. I've known others who fear the loss of all their wealth. I've seen some folks' faith get shaken just because their favorite politician didn't get elected and they feared terrible things would happen. What about you? What fears of the future are keeping you up at night?

One of the biggest robbers of our joy is the fear of the future. We cannot find satisfaction in our soul today when we are gnawing at our knuckles in worry about tomorrow.

Regret of the Past

A second huge robber of joy is our past. We can regret past mistakes and mess-ups so much that we fear to try again. The past chains us down so much that we can't even enjoy what's happening today. Failure or hurt or disappointment haunts us.

To be clear, we aren't talking about feeling bad about undealt-with sin. We should feel awful about our unrepented sins because the Holy Spirit is convicting us about those wrongs. But sometimes we've confessed and repented from our sins and yet they still chain us down. The past keeps us from enjoying today and looking forward to the future. We've lost joy to regret.

The people of Nehemiah's day almost missed out on the joy of "today" because they regretted their past.

Rejoicing in Today

In the book of Nehemiah, we read about the Jews returning to their promised land after so many decades away. While working on the wrecked city that had been the homeland of their parents and grandparents, they discovered a copy of the earlier sections of the Bible and were eager to learn more about the God of their ancestors. They set aside a time for a public reading of this just-found truth, and they listened intently. But as the words were read, it became clear that they hadn't been following God's way. It caused the people to weep as they realized their ignorance.

However, Nehemiah knew it wasn't time for mourning what had been missed in the past. Instead, he urged them to celebrate today:

> Nehemiah said, "Go and enjoy choice food and sweet drinks, and send some to those who have nothing prepared. This day is holy to our Lord. Do not grieve, for the **joy** of the Lord is your strength."
>
> The Levites calmed all the people, saying, "Be still, for this is a holy day. Do not grieve."
>
> Then all the people went away to eat and drink, to send portions of food and to celebrate with great **joy**, because they now understood the words that had been made known to them. (Nehemiah 8:10-14 NIV, emphasis added)

Regrets over their past sins almost robbed them of the joy of learning what God wanted of them now.

Throughout the book Nehemiah we also see attempts to use fear of the future to sap the joy and energy from God's people. Outsiders threaten and intimidate, trying to stop them. But God's people kept working, adjusting their schedules to add in a standing guard in case any of those threats were carried out. They were encouraged as they remembered all that God had done in their lives and throughout their history. (see Nehemiah 9) They kept going.

When all the work was finally done, then the people had a time of great celebration, filled with joy, for the city's walls were now rebuilt and they could stand strong against these intimidators. Read how Nehemiah describes it:

> "The two choirs that gave thanks then took their places in the house of God; so did I, together with half the officials, as well as the priests… …The choirs sang under the direction of Jezrahiah. And on that day they offered great sacrifices, **rejoicing** because God had given them great **joy**. The women and children also **rejoiced**. The sound of **rejoicing** in Jerusalem could be heard far away." (Nehemiah 9:40-43 NIV, emphasis added)

Their rejoicing was so loud, it probably intimidated those who had been trying to intimidate them.

Fight to Keep Your Joy

We may not be facing enemy troops or trying to rebuild a city wall, but all of us face obstacles that are trying to steal the joy out of our life, be it regrets from the past or fears of the future. We also need to realize that our kids are facing the same dilemma of stolen joy. They may not have as many years to regret nor as many layers of future-fears, but the loss of joy can be just as real for them. As parents, we need to fight for joy in our lives and teach our kids to do the same.

Joy doesn't just drop on us; joy must be pursued. Joy is a choice and sometimes it is a hard choice, but joy is always worth it. We need to trust the One who made us, that He can and will saturate us with joy as we focus on Him:

> "May the God of hope fill you with all **joy** and peace as you **trust in him**, so that you may overflow with hope by the power of the Holy Spirit." Romans 15:13 (NIV, emphasis added)

We can live a joyful life, no matter our circumstances. We don't have to wait until everything is perfect. We don't have to wait until we are millionaires. Instead, we only need to be aware of how regrets or fears can try to steal that away, and then we need to combat those "intimidaters" by trusting in God and getting on with a joyful life.

Daily Response

1. Regrets from the past can steal our joy for today. Are there any past decisions, sins, or mistakes that are robbing you of joy?

2. Fears of the future can also steal away our joy for today. What are some of the joy-stealing fears that you are facing now or have faced in the past?

3. Have you seen either regrets or fears robbing your childs' joy? How can you help them choose joy instead?

Gathering ending Week 2
Notes

The Fruit of Peace

But the fruit of the Spirit is love, joy, **peace**, forbearance, kindness, goodness, faithfulness, gentleness and self-control. Against such things there is no law. (Galatians 5:22-23 NIV *emphasis added*)

What is Peace?

Peace in the Storm

Eric: Amy and I started our life together with medical drama. The weekend after our engagement, both of her parents were in the hospital for different reasons. With every year after that, the hospital visits kept coming. We went to hospitals for good events (the births of our kids and friends' kids) and for terrible events (illnesses and injuries, surgeries and miscarriages). A few times we were the patients, but most of the time we were the visitors there to listen, console, advise, and pray. In our first dozen years together, Amy and I went to at least 17 different hospitals, and only a few of those were for 1 or 2 visits- most of those places we've been to multiple times. You would think we were trying to visit every hospital in Southern California.

Many times when we were dealing with medical emergencies of family or friends, we would experience his inner peace. It was like we were in the eye of the hurricane, calm even as the terrible storm whipped all around us. That was a God thing; he allowed us that peace so that we could be strong for others.

Everything is Whole

Peace is so much more than just the absence of fighting. In Christian teaching the concept of peace also includes the idea of rest, completion, reconciliation, wholeness, and being right with God and others. We are to have peace in our heart and in our relationships with others.

How important is peace for our Christian life? Well, consider that Paul thought it was so important that he started every one of his letters with a prayer for peace. Here's what he wrote in Romans 1:7: "To all in Rome who are loved by God and called to be his holy people: Grace and peace to you from God our Father and from the Lord Jesus Christ." The Apostle Peter does the same in his letters too, praying peace over the people. The apostles saw peace as an essential thing for us as believers.

So where does that peace come from and what does it look like in our lives?

Peace starts at the Cross

The reason that we have the opportunity to live a peace-filled life is because of what Jesus did for us:

> "For God was pleased to have all his fullness dwell in him, and through him to reconcile to himself all things, whether things on earth or things in heaven, by **making peace through his blood**, shed on the cross.
>
> "Once you were alienated from God and were enemies in your minds because of your evil behavior. But now **he has reconciled you** by Christ's physical body through death to present you holy in his sight, without blemish and free from accusation— if you continue in your faith, established and firm, and do not move from the hope held out in the gospel. This is the gospel that you heard and that has been proclaimed to every creature under heaven, and of which I, Paul, have become a servant."
> (Colossians 1:19-23 NIV- emphasis added)

God took the first step. Jesus reconciled us by sacrificing himself. The Lord provided the first and greatest reconciliation in our life when he brought wholeness to us by dying for our sins. For us or our children to have peace in our hearts, we must embrace his offer of salvation. We need to be willing to let him sacrifice himself for our wrongs. He brings peace to us, a wholeness and a sense of relief or release.

Peace Continues

God brought peace to our relationship with him through Jesus' sacrifice on the cross, and it does not end there. God continues to build that peace, that wholeness, that completeness, through the Holy Spirit who now lives in us:

> "The mind governed by the flesh is death, but the mind governed by
> the Spirit is life and peace."
> (Romans 8:6 NIV)

Our society wants to fill our minds with deadly ideas. We don't intend to sound paranoid, but at times it does feel like our society is after us and our children. Marketers want us to be envious or greedy so that we'll buy their stuff. Politicians want us to be outraged or fearful, so that we'll vote their way. So many want our money and allegiance. They want us dedicated to a brand or a political party or some superstar or a sport team, and they will appeal to our worst side, be that lust, anger, jealousy, or disdain for others. A mind caught up in all of this is a mind filled with deadly ideas.

What God is offering us instead is the chance to allow our mind to be governed by the Holy Spirit. When we allow God to be the boss of our mind, to rule it, then we will experience true life and real peace.

But even while writing this, I (Eric) lose my sense of peace as I feel that I need to work at submitting to God. Maybe that isn't your problem, but I often want to turn a promise from God into something that I must work at to bring about, which is why I need the reminder that follows below.

Peace for the Weary

Jesus promises to gently teach us and promises that we will find rest for our souls. He relates life to being oxen working in the field of life, wearing a yoke as we plow the field. Up one row and down the next, trudging along, maybe getting whipped to move faster as we struggle under the hot sun. But he promises a better life than that:

> "Come to me, all you who are weary and burdened, and I will give you rest. Take my yoke upon you and learn from me, for I am gentle and humble in heart, and you will find rest for your souls. For my yoke is easy and my burden is light." (Matthew 11:28-30 NIV)

Jesus isn't offering us a work-free, burden-free life, but he is offering one where the load seems easy and light. He says we will find rest for our souls- what a lovely promise. That inner turmoil, that uncertain restlessness, that fear, can all be put to rest. Life will still go and there will still be a field to plow but, by learning from him, we can go through life with an inner peace.

Peace for our Kids

We often think that is only the world-weary who hunger for peace, but even our kids desire it. They want peace at school, peace in the family, and a peaceful night of sleep without any scary monsters haunting their dreams. Unfortunately, we can't wrap our kids in bubble-wrap to protect them from all of life's bruisings. They will experience scares and disappointments, hurts and disagreements.

However, we can teach them about the inner peace that starts with knowing Jesus as their savior. Christian peace is not dependent on our circumstances; it is dependent on who we know and trust- Jesus.

Daily Response

1. If someone asked those around you (your coworkers, friends, or spouse) if peace rules your life, what would they say? Have they seen evidence of peace in you?

2. Would your kids consider you a peace-filled person?

3. How can you encourage your child to seek peace?

Reconciliation:
When We Mess Up

Words that Hurt

Eric: One of the most hurtful things I ever said happened when I was a young man talking with my dad. I forget why I was so furious with him, but I remember that we were standing at the bar in my parent's mobile home. (My parents liked creating a place to gather, so their family room was filled with a pool table, a sound system, a comfy couch, and a bar with a half-dozen stools.) On this occasion, it was just the two of us there, he behind the bar and me leaning on the padded front edge.

In my anger, I struck my dad with words that were more painful than any punch. **I told him that I was *disappointed* in him.** That word- disappointed- was brutal. I immediately saw the damage my words caused. His shocked face. His loss for words. It was a hard hit. Those were vicious words from me and he felt them deeply. I quickly realized it, but I was too angry and too proud to apologize or try to take them back.

My dad was a hard worker who did the best he could for his wife and kids. He immigrated from Germany to Canada with only a few dollars in his pocket, getting a job and saving up enough to bring my mom and my oldest three siblings over within a few months. A few years later, he immigrated to America. This time there were four children to bring along. Eventually my parents settled in California, where they had the last two of us kids. From nothing, my Vati worked his way up into the middle-class, often commuting long distances for work. He was a good yet flawed man. He certainly didn't deserve those harsh words from his youngest.

I really messed up as an adult kid, letting my anger drive me to say something very hurtful to my father.

Sadly, I only partially learned my lesson from that awful moment. I learned that I needed to watch my words, but I didn't learn that the power of my *tone* could be just as devastating.

Many years later and I was a dad myself. Once again, I was frustrated to the point of anger about something. I don't even remember what it was, but it was over my sons having done something after being told to stop doing it. Whatever brought it out of me, I yelled. My angry frustration came out in a loud, demanding voice that **sought to shame and intimidate them into correction**. It was powerful- for they stopped misbehaving and listened to me. It was scary- because my boys were looking at me with fear in their eyes as they saw a side of their dad they hadn't seen before.

Once again, I had messed up, but this time as a parent.

Parents Who Sin

Have you ever messed up as a parent? Have you sinned toward your children? Maybe anger isn't your trigger, but maybe your kids have experienced you breaking a promise, being crude, lying to them, cheating at a game, being selfish or neglectful, or maybe even forgetting them. The list of possible sins and mistakes is endless.

No matter how good a parent we are, we have messed up in our parenting and we will mess up again. It is kind of guaranteed because we are humans who still wrestle with sin.

Knowing that we have messed up in our past and will mess up again, we need to think about what we should do when it happens.

Will You Admit it or Deny it?

We all sin, but it can be very hard to admit to doing something wrong. We often claim to be innocent or act as if everything is fine when it really isn't. The Apostle John confronted that tendency in us when he wrote the following:

> This is the message we have heard from him and declare to you: God is light; in him there is no darkness at all. If we claim to have fellowship with him and yet walk in the darkness, we lie and do not live out the truth. But if we walk in the light, as he is in the light, we have fellowship with one another, and the blood of Jesus, his Son, purifies us from all sin.
>
> If we claim to be without sin, we deceive ourselves and the truth is not in us. If we confess our sins, he is faithful and just and will forgive us our sins and purify us from all unrighteousness. If we claim we have not sinned, we make him out to be a liar and his word is not in us.
>
> (1 John 1:5-10 NIV)

John mentions three false claims we might say, and then he tells us how to correct each one:

Claim #1 (1 John 1:6-7)- I'm good with God (even while I'm hip-deep in sins). I'm claiming that sin doesn't affect my relationship with God.

- **Truth of the Situation**- I'm lying and I'm not living out the truth.
- **Solution**- I need to change my behavior. Start walking in the light (doing right instead of sinning), then I'll have fellowship with others and Jesus will clean me up from my sins.

Claim #2 (1 John 1:8-9)- I'm done with sinning; it's no longer an issue for me. I'm claiming that I've had total victory over sin and I'm no longer tempted.

- **Truth of the Situation**- I'm deceiving myself and the Lord's truth isn't in me.
- **Solution**- I need to admit that I'm still doing wrong. If I confess my sins, he'll forgive me and clean me up.

Claim #3 (1 John 1:10)- I've never done anything wrong; I've never sinned. I'm claiming that I'm a good person who doesn't need any saving.

- **Truth of the Situation**- I'm calling Jesus a liar and I have no real relationship with him whatsoever.
- **Solution**- John doesn't offer me a solution. If this is me, then I obviously have nothing to do with Jesus.

Confess and Repent

When we mess up- and all of us will mess up and sin- we need to be quick to admit the wrong and correct what we are doing. We shouldn't let the sins linger; we shouldn't let the wrong go long without being righted.

When the sin is between us and our kids, it can be very hard to admit. Even if it was just something they witnessed, it is difficult to confess we messed up. We want to be a super hero in the eyes of our kids. We want to act like we never get anything wrong. We don't want to face the reality of our sinfulness and we don't want them to realize it about us either, but the truth is that they already know. The truth is, they will probably have more respect for us if we are honest and confess our wrongs and then change.

"I'm sorry." Those are powerful words that Amy has taught me, Eric, to use far more freely. Amy is very quick to apologize. (I've joked that she'll even apologize for the wrongs that I do.) She likes to keep short accounts- to get things right as quickly as possible and restore the harmony. My wife has taught me the importance of dealing with my sin as quickly as possible, especially when that sin has caused a rift with others- even if those "others" are our children. Those words- I'm sorry- can change everything when we use them sincerely with our kids.

I had to get things right with my dad after I used those hurtful words with him. Thankfully, I was able to reconcile with him, and in the last years of his life I even had the blessing of seeing him become a Christian.

I also had to confess the sin of anger to my kids after I yelled at them, although at first I tried to justify my sin but pointing at their sins (have you ever done that, or is it just me that tries that?). Finally, I admitted my wrong to them and asked for their forgiveness. Have I been the perfect dad since then? Obviously not, but whenever I've sinned against them or in their presence, I have tried to be quick to confess and repent- first seeking peace with God and then with them.

We must confess first to God because any sin is first against our Lord. Second, we confess to the other person we wronged, especially if it is our kid. Finally, we repent- which means we stop doing the wrong and start doing the right.

Daily Response

1. Has anyone you've respected ever apologized to you? (A parent, teacher, pastor, good friend, mentor, etc.) How did it feel to have them admit their error?

2. Have you ever apologized to your children? How did they receive it?

3. If we were to ask your kids what your worst sins are, what would they say?

Reconciliation:

When our Kids Mess Up

My Kid is Human

Amy: My kids sin. I've got great kids, but they still mess up. Sometimes they just do something stupid or have an accident. Sometimes they purposely disobey or flaunt one of our household rules. We first realized that our eldest wasn't perfect during a Christmas shopping trip when he had his first toddler temper tantrum. My sweet boy suddenly turned into an angry, screaming two-year-old, on the floor yelling and crying because we hadn't gone to the toy section. At first, I didn't know what to do. In the end, we picked him up and carried him out- our shopping excursion cut short.

They All Do It

How many of us have children who have done something wrong? From a preschooler throwing their food across the room, to a teen participating in drugs or alcohol, there are so many ways that they can blow it. What is the Biblical response?

Mistakes, Accidents, and Sins

One of the best-known parables from Jesus is the one about the Prodigal Son. Most of the time when we read or hear that story, we imagine ourselves as either the prodigal or as the older son, but have you ever imagined yourself as the dad? When Jesus told these stories, he wanted us to put ourselves into each role and learn from them.

Let's read it and try putting ourselves into that parent role that we usually assign to God:

> "Jesus continued: "There was a man who had two sons. The younger one said to his father, 'Father, give me my share of the estate.' So he divided his property between them."" (Luke 15:11-12 NIV)

How would you feel if your kid told you he couldn't wait for you to die- that he wanted his inheritance now? Would you be willing to give him his share early? The son was planning to move far away and wanted the money to start a new life. At that distance, he probably expected to have no more contact with his family and wouldn't be around when his father grew old and eventually passed away. Imagine your kid telling you that he was moving to another country and would never come back, so let him have his inheritance now.

The dad could have denied his request. He could have disinherited him out of spite. Instead, the dad took the time to split up his estate and did just what his son wanted, even though he probably didn't like it.

Take a moment to read the rest of the story in Luke 15:13-32.

The son really messed up his attempt at a new life. He made terrible friends and even worse decisions. He partied and wasted all that wealth. His dad had worked hard for many years to build up that fortune and the son blew through it far too quickly. Soon, the large stash of money disappeared and he found himself all alone. A famine came to the area and the young man found himself starving and without a place to live. The son went from living the life of a celebrity to being a wretch who hungered for pig slop.

Maybe you've faced something similar as a parent. Any kid can mess it up just as badly as the prodigal son: loose living, drugs, problems with the law, unemployment, single parenthood, terrible friends, and so on. If so, then you can really relate to this story. But even if your kid is too young for that much rebellion or has been an overall good kid, you will still face those moments when they mess up somehow. It will happen.

They've Admitted their Sin. Now What?

Every kid will mess up. That's guaranteed. Usually, there will also come a time when they realize that they have sinned. It might take a few hours for them to realize that coloring the walls with crayons is wrong. It might take a few years before they will admit that moving in to their friend's party house was a bad decision.

We aren't talking about a kid who simply had a moment of feeling bad about the consequences of his sin. The prodigal really repented. It wasn't easy for him to leave that foreign country and travel all that distance back home when he no longer had a wad of money to pay for first-class transport. He repented and took the risk of going home, expecting to live the life of a servant at-best, and no longer as a cherished son.

The wait for a child to repent can even last longer than your life. I (Amy) had an uncle who really rebelled against his Christian upbringing. He became an alcoholic, spent many nights in jail, married a drug dealer, and disowned his parents (my grandparents). And yet his parents and their friends kept praying for him. For years. For decades. It wasn't until years after my grandparents had died, that he realized his wrongs. My uncle ended up on the back pew of a small church weeping every Sunday, truly repenting. He chose to be baptized and all of his long-time friends and relatives saw a marked change. He truly was a new creation in Christ. About six months later he had a tragic bicycling accident and passed away. God answered those years of praying and my uncle had that opportunity to clearly see his need for his Savior.

Hopefully, your child will eventually realize their error just as the prodigal did. Once they do, then you'll have a tough decision to make.

The question is how will you react to their sin or mistake or accident or failure when they finally admit they messed up. Let's see how the prodigal's dad reacted.

> ""But while he was still a long way off, his father saw him and was filled with compassion for him; he ran to his son, threw his arms around him and kissed him."
> (Luke 15: 20 NIV)

We need to learn from the father. We should be excited at their new life and rejoice with them over their new freedom because they are no longer the same person. They've changed.

The dad welcomed his son home with a hug and a kiss. When your kids blow it and then come back to you, do you lecture or do you love? Do you hold-at-a-distance or do you hug? Do you run to them, welcoming them back, or do you cross your arms and demand penance?

Celebrate Repentance

The son admitted that he sinned against God and his dad, but when he tried to go on with his memorized speech his dad interrupted and called for a celebration.

When your kid finally comes clean about who shaved the dog or who dented the minivan or who broke the vacuum, do you celebrate their confession? Would you take them out for an ice cream after they admitted their sin?

We need to realize that our kids build a picture of God based on how we treat them. If we want them to realize that God is loving and forgiving, then we need to be that way with them. If we want them to know that God loves reconciliation, then they need to see us being quick to reconcile.

Daily Response

1. How do you usually react when your kid confesses to doing something wrong? Is there anything you can do better in your response?

2. "Our kids build a picture of God based on how we treat them." How do you feel about this statement? Can you see examples of this truth in your life and how your parents formed your picture of God? How can you improve the picture of God you're presenting to your kids?

3. Jesus' story is focused on celebrating the recovery of the lost. This is a suite of three parables that he told after people complained about him welcoming sinners and eating with them. His first story is about a lost sheep, where the owner leaves his 99 safe sheep because that lost one is still important. When he finds it, he rejoices and invites everyone else to join in his rejoicing. The second story is about a lost coin and how the owner worked through the night searching for it and then she celebrated its recovery. With all three stories, Jesus is encouraging us to celebrate when the lost are recovered and when the sinner repents. How can you celebrate when your kids repent? Who else can you invite into the celebration?

Being a Peacemaker

Them are Fightin' Words!

Eric: When I was a young and single guy, I had a friend who loved to argue. No matter what opinion you expressed, he would find a way to disagree with you. He never sought compromise or agreement. Instead, he was always determined to win. Whether it was an opinion about politics, food, sports, religion, or even the weather, he was sure that his viewpoint was the right one. Even if your opinion was close to his own, he would still argue against you. There was no "meeting in the middle" with him.

But I don't want you to have the impression that my friend was the only one who was causing strife. I have to admit that I often had fun "poking the bear" by saying things just to get him arguing. With just a few comments, I could keep him going for an hour.

We were just a couple of single guys killing a weekend afternoon with useless heated discussion. Neither of us was being a peacemaker. His argumentative ways might be more apparent and were certainly louder, but my calm baiting was just as destructive. I was making mischief, not peace. I was creating discord by setting him off.

Makers of Strife or Peace?

Maybe you've never baited someone into arguing, but most likely you've done other things to disrupt the peace. Some of us are loud and obvious with our peace disruption: yelling, mocking, accusing, embarrassing, bullying, and so on. Some of us are quieter but just as disruptive: gossiping, shunning, tempting, lying, implying, and more.

We often find a twisted sense of satisfaction from stirring trouble. We convince ourselves that the other person deserved it.

- Of course, I cut him off. He shouldn't have been trying to merge his car in front of me!
- Yes, I embarrassed her, but it was for her own good; she shouldn't have been doing something so stupid.
- I wasn't really gossiping because what I shared was true.

We often justify our strife making, seeing it as standing up for principles or as a way to defend ourselves. But God calls us and our children into a different life role: he doesn't call us to make strife or spread lies. He calls us to bring peace.

Peace of Jesus

We bring peace to others by introducing them to the good news of Jesus. When Paul describes our "spiritual armor" he mentions the shoes that complete the outfit: "and with your feet fitted with the readiness that comes from the gospel of peace." (Ephesians 6:15 NIV) We need to realize that the message of Jesus is one of bringing peace between that person and the Lord.

Here are a few more verses that describe why we should pursue peace:

"Blessed are the peacemakers, for they will be called children of God." (Matthew 5:9 NIV)

"Make every effort to live in peace with everyone and to be holy; without holiness no one will see the Lord." (Hebrews 12:14 NIV)

"If it is possible, as far as it depends on you, live at peace with everyone." (Romans 12:18 NIV)

As Christians, we are to make the effort to live in peace with everyone. The world around us might be thriving on offense and argument and anger, but we aren't supposed to be like the world. We are to mend and make whole, not tear apart. We are to bring together, not separate or shun. We are to invite them to meet Jesus, not declare them an enemy.

Making Peace

"But the wisdom that comes from heaven is first of all pure; then peace-loving, considerate, submissive, full of mercy and good fruit, impartial and sincere. Peacemakers who sow in peace reap a harvest of righteousness." (James 3:17-18 NIV)

Making peace is not done passively. We don't bring peace by avoiding the problems. We don't bring peace by permitting misbehavior to continue. We do bring peace through wisdom, and that comes by having the right attitude (peace-loving, considerate, submissive), having the right equipment (full of mercy and good fruit), and having the right approach (impartial and sincere).

Making peace can be harder than making strife. Making peace is building up, completing, lovingly correcting, and providing rest. Most importantly, making peace is bringing the good news of Jesus to that other person.

Daily Response

1. How are you as a peacemaker?

2. How are you at making peace in your home? Do your kids know you as a strife maker or as a peace maker?

3. How can you teach and model peacemaking to your kids?

Praying as a Parent

Emergency Prayer

Amy: Neither of my pregnancies were easy, but with my youngest we almost lost him just before he was born. The umbilical cord was wrapped around his neck, causing his heart rate to greatly fluctuate with each contraction. The doctor even prepped me for an emergency cesarean, ordering Eric out of the room. My husband was outside, pacing the hallway, praying fervently for me and our child, as I struggled to give birth. In my pain and exhaustion, I didn't realize how dire the situation was, but Eric did and he prayed.

Pray without Ceasing

Sometimes praying for our kids is forced on us by a life-or-death situation. We can really become fervent in our desperation. That's good, because God can and does intervene during the darkest of times. But we also need to be praying for our children on ordinary days.

We should be praying *for* our kids and *with* our kids every day. Praying for future spouses, future grandkids, and future life as an adult. Praying 10 -20 years into their future, and also praying for their next wobbly step. Prayer should be a daily habit, but that's so hard to do in our overly busy lives. They need our prayers but it's hard to prioritize the time in our distracted days.

Our kids, no matter their age, are facing an increasingly hostile world where Christian morals are seen as antique and irrelevant. They are being taught by schools, by society, and by social media the antithesis of Christianity: where right is wrong, and bad is good.

Praying the Lord's Prayer over our Kids

Praying for our kids is a great daily practice, but sometimes it's hard to know where to start. Well, a great beginning when praying for our kids is the Lord's Prayer (Matthew 6:9-13). Most Christians have memorized these verses but we often don't notice that it isn't a "me" prayer. This is an "us" prayer. It's a prayer for a group instead of just for ourself. Try doing a word replacement in this passage, switching every "us/we/our" to the names of your children.

> "This, then, is how you should pray:
> " '**Our** Father in heaven,
> hallowed be your name,
> your kingdom come,
> your will be done,
> on earth as it is in heaven.
> Give **us** today **our** daily bread.
> And forgive **us our** debts,
> as **we** also have forgiven **our** debtors.
> And lead **us** not into temptation,
> but deliver **us** from the evil one.'
> (Matthew 6:9-13 NIV, emphasis added)

By praying this prayer for our kids, we are praying for provision, forgiveness, direction, and protection. We acknowledge that God is their father just as much as we are their parent- and the Father can fill in where we come up short. We ask God to provide their daily needs. We ask Him to forgive their debts/ shortcomings/ trespasses even as our kids forgive those who owe them. We ask God to keep them away from areas of temptation and testing that is too much for them, but to instead get them away from the evil one.

Pray the Prayer of BLESSing

Another way to start praying for your kids daily is to do the BLESS prayer. This is a prayer for 5 things, each represented by a letter in the word BLESS. It takes only a few minutes but it can be powerful. I (Amy) pray this over my kids every morning before going to work.

B- bodily health. Pray for their physical well-being.

L- labor. Pray for their work, whether that's a job or school.

E- emotional. Pray for their emotional health.

S- social. Pray for their friendships and other relationships.

S- spiritual. Pray for their spiritual health.

Modeling Prayer to our Kids

Not only do we need to be praying for our kids, we also need to model praying in front of them. They need to develop their own prayer life because our God is very relational. He wants that communication with them. He wants them to be looking to him for comfort, wisdom, direction, and love.

Invite your kids to pray before a meal or at bedtime. Develop those routines that can become a habit of seeking out God. God wants our kids to see him as their friend. (Think of Jesus wanting the little children to come to him.) As their relationship with God grows, it will mature into a deeper understanding of God.

Daily Response

1. How is your prayer life right now? Are you regularly praying for your kids?

2a. If you haven't been praying daily for your kids, start small. Which of the above models would work for you? The Lord's Prayer or the Prayer of BLESSing?

2b. If you are praying regularly for your kids and with your kids, what can you do to make it more meaningful?

3. Are your kids praying regularly? How can you empower them to pray more? (like letting them lead family prayer or teaching them to pray for others)

Gathering ending Week 3
Notes

SPECIAL GATHERING

Praise and Prayer Experience

After about three weeks of going through *Jesus Embraced Parenting*, it is time to gather to pray. This is a time to praise every child and to pray for all the kids by name.

> **Where and When?** This is a separate gathering from your usual weekly meeting, done sometime during week 3 or 4. We recommend picking a quieter location where there's also room to spread out for individual prayer. Possible meeting locations: someone's home, at church, or at a neighborhood park.
>
> It is highly recommended that the group finish this experience with a shared meal, like a fast-food lunch in the park, a backyard barbecue, or a potluck dinner.

Fasting in Preparation: We encourage all participants to fast for a time before the Praise and Prayer Experience. The idea of fasting is to deny yourself something as a way to focus your mind and sharpen your spiritual awareness. Many choose to give up eating (fasting a meal or a full day before the event), but others might choose to *fast* technology, social media, coffee, sweets, or some other favorite activity. The idea is to take the time you would usually be doing this activity and pray during that time instead.

During your fast, focus your prayer time on your children, asking God to show you specific things about them.

Consider inviting your kids to join you in fasting, especially if they are elementary age or older. The coming Praise and Prayer Experience is about them, so it would be good to get them involved in this too. Obviously, adjust the fasting to be age appropriate for them.

Prepare Your Praise Cards: Your group leader should have handed out index cards about a week before this gathering, one card for each of your kids. You should take the time to write praises.

Prepare your Prayer Requests: Come to the meeting with prayer requests for each child. It should be something you and your child feel comfortable sharing in front of others.

If it's of a sensitive nature, consider doing a more generalized request.

Child involvement: If possible, have all the children that belong to the group present for the Praise and Prayer Experience. We realize that this isn't always doable because of life situations. We want to be sensitive that not all parents/ guardians/ grandparents/ mentors will have their children with them on that particular day. Nonetheless, all kids should be prayed for by name, whether they are present or not.

Childcare during the event: You may want to consider having someone available to watch younger kids during the gathering when those children are not being praised or prayed over to prevent distractions.

Praise and Prayer Experience

1. **Group Start** (large group circle) (15-20 minutes)
   - Begin with a Scripture reading about prayer. (This is your choice, but some good options are Psalm 8, Psalm 34, Psalm 103, and/or Psalm 128.)
   - Talk about what prayer is and why it is important in our lives. Share what the group hopes to accomplish during this Praise and Prayer Experience.
   - "Whatever is shared in the group should stay in the group." There should be a reminder about confidentiality, since the children aren't usually present and most (if not all) are minors.

2. **Praising Each Child** (large group circle) (15-30 minutes, depending on size of group and number of kids present)
   - Taking turns, each parent reads aloud (in front of everyone) their Praise Card for their kid(s). Try to keep your praise statements to less than 2 minutes per child.
   - We would suggest saving your cards for your kids. They may want them now, or you may want to save them to bring out at some later time to remind them of what you wrote.

3. **Prayer Circles** (small group circles) (15-30 minutes, depending on the size of the group and number of kids)
   - Break up into groups with 2-3 families in each group. This is a time for adults to pray over every child in that small group (and pray in proxy for any kids not there).

- Encourage kids to join in praying for the others.
- Please focus your time on the kids.
- Laying on of hands is optional, but can make the experience more meaningful. Just be aware that some children might not want to be touched or might be intimidated by grown-ups crowding around them. Respect each kid (and adult); we want this to be an affirming experience and not a weird or uncomfortable one.

4. **Return to Large Group**: (5-15 minutes) Once the small group prayer time is done, gather back together as a large group.
   - Once the small group time is done, gather back together as a large group.
   - Have about 2 or 3 people finish your prayer time. If any are willing, have the kids pray.

5. **Meal and Celebration**: (about an hour) Close off your time together with a shared meal. This is your chance to break your fast and talk about the prayer experience. How did you hear God during the prayer time? Did your fasting help you prepare for praying? Did fasting make the prayer time feel more vibrant or special?

The Fruit of Forbearance (Patience)

But the fruit of the Spirit is love, joy, peace, **forbearance**, kindness, goodness, faithfulness, gentleness and self-control. Against such things there is no law. (Galatians 5:22-23 NIV *emphasis added*)

What is Patience?

Patience with Little Hands

Eric: "Daddy, I want to help." Those words can bring a smile and a sigh at the same time. With young kids, "helping" means that the job will take 2-3 times longer. Whether it is cooking, cleaning, repairing, or yard work, you need patience with your helper because they aren't as strong or skilled as you, but they are eager to try.

As preschoolers, hand washing dirty dishes was very fascinating to our kids because it involved water and bubbles and brushes. What could be more fun than that? In our first house together, Amy and I didn't have a dishwasher- just our hands- and I remember getting those offers of assistance.

"Daddy, I want to help wash the dishes."

The offer of help was sincere and I wanted to encourage the desire to help out, but it meant dish washing was going to double in time. First, I needed to arrange a stool or chair so that they could reach the sink. Next, I had to designate a job- usually the initial wash and brushing, so that I could finish cleaning anything that made it through that first "wash cycle" and was still dirty. I taught them how to handle fragile glassware, how to scrub harder in pots, and to clean both the inside and the outside of everything. Did they remember much of those instructions afterwards? Not really. They just remembered the splashing, the tiny bubbles floating up from the foam, and working with the sponges and cleaning brushes. Maybe it was best that they only remembered the fun parts, since that made them more willing to volunteer again.

It takes time to train apprentice dishwashers. It takes patience.

Forbearance is not Optional

Depending on the Bible translation you are reading, it could be using the word "forbearance" instead of "patience". Both words project a good picture of what God is asking of us here. These days, forbearance is mainly used in the financial sector to describe a temporary pause in loan payments: the bank agrees to wait on its monthly collections. It willingly delays to allow the borrower extra time to raise the money. We are being told to live that way too, to willingly delay so that others have more time.

Being patient is not an easy trait for many of us. We live in a world that always seems to be rushing around us, a culture that encourages selfishness and impatience. In the business world, it often can become cut-throat as people battle for the next bonus, sale, or promotion. We get impatient with our kids, wondering why it takes them so long to grasp reading or tying their shoes or brushing their hair.

So much around us is screaming "think only about yourself", "don't wait for others", and "you deserve instant gratification", and yet as Christians we're taught that patience is vital. How do we reconcile that? How do we resist the voices of our selfish society and embrace Christian forbearance? How do we slow down for our kids? How do we teach our children to be patient with others?

The Friends of Patience

The Apostle Paul had a driven personality and at times was rather blunt with others. He wasn't one to put up with fools or slackers. He endured beatings and prison, shipwrecks and injuries. He confronted spiritual leaders and powerful rulers, and yet he also learned the importance of getting along with others and the need for Christian harmony:

> As a prisoner for the Lord, then, I urge you to live a life worthy of the calling you have received. Be completely humble and gentle; be patient, bearing with one another in love. Make every effort to keep the unity of the Spirit through the bond of peace. (Ephesians 4:1-3 NIV)

If you have ever watched any cooking shows, you've probably heard about foods that fit well together- pairing a drink with an entrée or matching certain sauces to particular meats. Well, in the above verses Paul is giving us a good list of traits that pair well with patience:

- Humility
- Gentleness
- Being Loving in our forbearance
- Striving for Unity of the Spirit

Each of these traits aren't the same as patience but they do complement patience. Humility and patience fit well together, as do *gentleness* and *being loving* and *unity*. All these traits are like a group of friends who, when they come together, bring out the best in each other.

What does it look like to go the Way of Patience? It looks like us being humble, gentle, lovingly forbearing, and working hard for Holy Spirit unity. Patience is allowing the other person to take the necessary time. Patience is being willing to wait. Patience endures through hard times and even through attacks, knowing that something better lies ahead.

Asking for Patience

I've heard people share that we should never ask God to teach us how to be patient because he will do so! They were implying that awful things will happen if you pray for patience- that God will put you through the wringer to squeeze as much painful patience as possible out of you. Such a teaching is superstitious nonsense and it draws God as some kind of mean fellow who likes to torture us. That's a false picture of God. Does he want to teach us how to be patient? Yes! Because he understands that we need patience to survive and thrive in this world. We need patience to walk in the Spirit.

Our children need patience too, especially while learning new skills and conquering new tasks. They need patience to master the Third Grade and also to master a three-point shot in basketball. They need it to balance a bank account and also to balance on a log crossing the stream. They will especially need forbearance to develop friends and build relationships. If we don't model and teach them patience, then they will give up on so many things before they get the chance to experience success in that area.

The fruit of forbearance needs to be nurtured and tended to produce the best crop in our life. We should want to be more patient in our Christian walk, especially toward our children. We should also want to teach them the importance of patience, because they are followers of Jesus too.

Daily Response

1. How is your patience toward your kid(s)? What are areas where you can improve?

2. Take a moment and think of your child's life. Are there any areas where they are good at being patient? How can you encourage them to get even better in those areas?

3. What are some areas where your child can grow in patience? How can you model patience to them? How can you teach them to embrace patience?

True Friendship

Friendship Betrayed

Amy: One of the greatest hurts in life is when a friend abandons you. I'm not talking about a friend disappointing you or angering you or arguing with you. Any friendship of length and depth will have its share of occasional turbulence. I'm talking about friends who suddenly decide to end that friendship.

In kindergarten, I met this girl (let's call her Anne) who I had a lot in common with: we were both only kids, our birthdays were just a day apart, and we both liked the same games. We became quick friends and remained close all the way through seventh grade. Even our moms became friends because Anne and I were together so much. But in the spring of our eighth grade, during a field trip, a mutual friend told me that Anne had confessed that she planned to drop me as a friend. I wasn't cool enough for her. Hearing that hurt, but it confirmed what I had already sensed. Anne and I were drifting apart. By high school, our friendship was over.

Real Friends

Being a true friend takes time, because it requires experiencing life together and proving your sincerity, affection, and integrity to each other. We (Amy and Eric) are true friends to each other as well as being married. We also have a double handful of others we consider true friends who we can depend on because they love us and really want to see the best in our lives.

All of us want our kids to have true friends who will bring out the best in them. Our children need friends who will do life with them, during the laughing and the crying, during the fun and the serious. So how can we model true friendship to them and teach our kids how to make and be a real friend?

Jesus Shows the Way

Jesus modeled to us what true friendship is like. Read what he said about being friends:

"As the Father has loved me, so have I loved you. Now remain in my love. If you keep my commands, you will remain in my love, just as I have kept my Father's commands and remain in his love. I have told you this so that my joy may be in you and that your joy may be complete. My command is this: Love each other as I have loved you. Greater love has no one than this: to lay down one's life for one's friends. You are my friends if you do what I command. I no longer call you servants, because a servant does not know his master's business. Instead, I have called you friends, for everything that I learned from my Father I have made known to you. You did not choose me, but I chose you and appointed you so that you might go and bear fruit—fruit that will last—and so that whatever you ask in my name the Father will give you. This is my command: Love each other. (John 15:9-17 NIV)

Jesus offers his friendship, a love so great that it culminates in his sacrifice for us. He promises to share with us everything he's learned from the Father. But he also calls us to our part of this joyful friendship: we are to go out, bear fruit that lasts, and (most importantly) love each other. This is not simply a one-on-one friendship. This is a friendship where we need to invite in all others who also have been befriended by Jesus.

He is inviting us into friendships that take time to develop. Look back at the Bible passage above and notice how often Jesus uses the words "remain", "keep", "know", and "last". Those words all imply a lengthy time period. He's inviting us into deep and loving and lifelong friendship with him and with all the other believers around us.

These are the kind of true friends we desire for ourselves and the kind of friendships we hope our children develop. They don't happen overnight; they take time to grow, but they are so worth it.

Friends for the Long Haul

When I (Amy) went to high school, I made other friends who filled that gap from losing Anne. I made even more friends during my college years. With many of them, we are still close almost thirty years later. Some of us have even talked about what it would be like growing old together, setting our rocking chairs next to each other at the old folks' home.

Our kids need to learn what's a true friend, just as I had to with Anne. For them to learn, they need it modeled by us. Are we working on building real friendships or are we too busy or scared to go beyond casual acquaintances? Are we allowing people into our inner circle of friends who lift us up or are they people who use or abuse us? It's okay to limit who can gets close; its okay to be selective. Frankly, its necessary to have appropriate boundaries with our developing friendships, because we need friendships that are healthy.

We don't just model friendship to our kids, but we also need to teach them how to recognize a potential good friend. That could mean asking them questions when they make new acquaintances, getting them to think about how they're being treated and how they are treating others in return. We need to teach our kids that true friendship takes time and effort. In our society with anonymous online "friends" and instant followers and immediate feedback, it can be hard to learn the patience needed to build real friends.

Daily Response

1. How does patience help with your friendships?

2. How can you model building better friendships to your child?

3. How can you teach them to be a better friend to others?

Perseverance

Enduring the Early Years

Eric: We learned a lot about perseverance when we became parents. Who doesn't remember how wonderful it was to get a full night sleep after enduring weeks or months of sleep deprivation caused by a newborn's demand for milk every few hours? When that baby finally slept for four hours, then six, then eight, oh it was glorious. Sleep, wonderful sleep!

Another trying time for us was potty training. One of our boys stubbornly refused to use the toilet to go #2. He kept fighting it well into his third year, refusing to give up those diapers. Why stop playing when you can just poop in your pants and keep going? It was a routine that was familiar and comfortable to him (as much as a stinky diaper can ever be comfortable). Our son had no medical or developmental reason for the delay- he just didn't want to poop in the toilet.

Amy, who was taking the lead in his toilet training, got so frustrated that one day she actually wondered if she was the world's worst mom. How come some parents made this potty training stuff seem like a breeze? What are we doing wrong? Will he ever get this or are we going to be sending him to college in diapers? She was convinced that she was a horrible mother because she couldn't get our son fully potty trained.

What are Your Fights?

It can be hard to persevere and stick with something when you are strongly opposed, even when what you're struggling with is a child's stubbornness. Looking back, Amy and I can laugh at the potty training fight (ADULT VS. PRESCHOOLER: WHO WILL WIN THE BATTLE OF WILLS?) but, when we were in the middle of it, the struggle was very real.

The toilet wars are now long behind us, but parenting brings new battles each year, over food choices, screen time, chores, bedtime, and so on.

In addition to parenting struggles, we have face plenty more at work, at home, in the neighborhood, with family or friends or co-workers. Things can seem overwhelming at times, making us want to quit or cry or rage or look for an escape. Even today as you read this, you may be worn out from persevering, tired and feeling dejected. So how does God encourage us to keep going?

Patiently Waiting

In the letter from James, he relates our endurance to the waiting that every farmer must go through:

> Be patient, then, brothers and sisters, until the Lord's coming. See how the farmer waits for the land to yield its valuable crop, patiently waiting for the autumn and spring rains. You too, be patient and stand firm, because the Lord's coming is near. Don't grumble against one another, brothers and sisters, or you will be judged. The Judge is standing at the door!
>
> Brothers and sisters, as an example of patience in the face of suffering, take the prophets who spoke in the name of the Lord. As you know, we count as blessed those who have persevered. You have heard of Job's perseverance and have seen what the Lord finally brought about. The Lord is full of compassion and mercy. (James 5:7-11 NIV)

Eventually, there will be an end to every struggle, even if the end comes with our death. The Apostle Paul endured his "thorn in the flesh" for the rest of his life as far as we know. Many people have to persevere with chronic illness or the ongoing urges of past addictions. Some, like those James addresses above, face ongoing persecution and suffering. However, even if it goes for a lifetime, he urges us to be patient and stand firm. He wants us to keep our focus in the right direction, not on the problems but on our Lord who is compassionate and merciful and will return.

Keep Going

Our Perseverance with our son did pay off; he mastered potty training. Actually, he mastered it the very next day, after Amy's declaration that she was the world's worst mom for not getting him trained. So in 24 hours, Amy went from "worst" to "best" because he not only started pooping in the toilet, he never went back to doing it in his pants. Our long battle ended in victory!

Persevering is not something we usually celebrate, at least not until AFTER we get through it. We celebrate reaching our weight goal, but during the struggle to lose those pounds we are gritting our teeth. We celebrate mastering a new work skill or athletic move or technical ability, but during that learning curve we are sweating the details. We celebrate a court judgment in our favor, but we weren't happy during the months of defending our innocence.

Persevering is an uncomfortable type of patience; it is a type of patience where we are having to endure. With perseverance, we have to keep looking toward the end goal, which as Christians is our uniting with our Lord and being in his presence, face-to-face.

Daily Response

1. As a parent, what are you having to persevere through right now?

2. What are your children having to persevere through right now?

3. How can you help your children learn the importance of persevering?

Mentoring our Kids

Teaching the Basics

Eric: During our early parenting years, Amy and I weren't very good at instructing our kids in the Christian faith, especially in teaching them about the Bible. Using our busy lives as an excuse, we had left too much of the teaching to Sunday School teachers and Christian animated videos and Christian music. We both knew better, but still neglected mentoring our kids in the ways of Jesus. It was just so hard to find the time.

One evening I was talking with a good friend who had recently returned to active Christianity after a split with his wife. He had grown up in a Christian family and had known all the Bible stories from a young age, but had wandered away from the faith as an adult after some rather hurtful church experiences, a rocky marriage, and then a divorce. As a result, his own kids were rather ignorant about the faith.

Now that my friend had returned to Jesus, he wanted his children to learn the stories that he had known growing up. So, even though his three were already teenagers, he bought an illustrated children's Story Bible and they began reading it as a family, using it as a discussion starter.

I was convicted and inspired by my friend's commitment to his kids. He had shown that he was willing to take the time for them.

No Time for Mentoring our Kids

Too often we expect our kids to learn how to follow Jesus by simply "catching it" from being around church meetings and Christian family, but most likely we would all agree that's not the best strategy. Yet we struggle to do what's right.

Life just seems too busy and the days too short. Where can we find the time to do this and where would we even start?

Submitting to our Kids

Paul the Apostle, in his letter to the believers in Ephesus, states a radical concept: that we are all to be in submission to one another. It doesn't matter what your wealth or social status- we are called to submit, and to do so out of our love and respect for Jesus.

> Submit to one another out of reverence for Christ.
> (Ephesians 5:21 NIV)

Paul then talks about three of the most power-imbalanced relationships that the Ephesian church goers were likely to encounter: 1) husband and wife, 2) father and child, and 3) master and slave. We will focus on that second relationship.

In those days of the Roman Empire, children had to obey their parents no matter what, especially their father. If a dad wanted to beat his kids or even maim them, there was no law against it. The father held his child's life in his hands; he had the right to make any decision he wanted concerning his kid.

Into that society, Paul spoke these revolutionary words about mutual submission, explaining what it looks like in such an imbalanced relationship:

> Children, obey your parents in the Lord, for this is right. "Honor your father and mother"—which is the first commandment with a promise— "so that it may go well with you and that you may enjoy long life on the earth."
>
> Fathers, do not exasperate your children; instead, bring them up in the training and instruction of the Lord. (Ephesians 6:1-4 NIV)

So what does it look like for parents to submit to their kids? To submit to our children, we should never exasperate them. Exasperate means to irritate or frustrate intensely. As parents, especially when our kids are younger, we have the power to easily exasperate them. We can cruelly tease, break promises, deny their wants, ignore their needs, refuse to listen to them, and so much more. We have the power to exasperate and society might see nothing wrong in us doing so, but we need to resist that selfish and cruel approach to parenting. Don't do it.

We are also told to raise them in the ways of Jesus. We are to train and instruct. Once again, that is submitting to them and their spiritual needs. It takes time to mentor and teach another. There is a lot of patience that goes into bringing up our children in the truths of Jesus, and this is a task that we really can't farm out to others. We shouldn't depend on a Sunday School teacher, a youth pastor, a babysitter, a nanny, a grandparent, or anyone else to "bring them up in the training and instruction of the Lord." We can use their help, of course, but those others aren't with our kids as much as we are. *We* need to do the training and instructing. *We* are the ones who need to patiently model what it means to follow Jesus.

Modeling what it means to be a Christian

That single dad who saw a gap in his kids' spiritual instruction was creative in how he solved it. Maybe you don't need to read an illustrated Bible to your kids, but are there any other gaps in your kids' training and instruction that you need to take the time to fill?

As parents, we have a huge responsibility of showing our kids what Christianity is all about. We model it in our daily habits and routines. Do they see us praying or thanking God? Do we pray as a family before meals or at bedtime? Do we model charity and forgiveness? Have we taught them the basics of the faith and shared with them the stories of the Bible?

Teaching our kids the ways of Jesus is something that happens day-after-day, as the years pass. We need to patiently bring them up in the faith. They may rebel someday like the prodigal son, but we need to do our part.

Daily Response

1. What are some things you have done to bring your kids "up in the training and instruction of the Lord"?

2. What Christian routines do you have as a family? (Praying for others, giving to the needy, attending church gatherings, etc.) How involved are your kids in those routines?

3. Do you need to improve your submitting to your children, either in the areas of exasperating or in training and instructing? What could you do better?

Enduring Suffering

Enduring Scoliosis

Amy: Back in my teen years, I was diagnosed with scoliosis (curvature of the spine) and was put in a back brace for over a year to try to correct the issue but it didn't work. Not only was I getting teased for my hunched-up back but also for my not-so-hidden brace. My best friend at the time deserted me, too embarrassed to be seen with someone with a physical deformity.

So the summer between middle school and high school I went in for an extreme back surgery where they inserted steel rods inside me to straighten my spine. The surgery, delayed by a major earthquake here in Southern California, took eight hours. My recovery took three months with intense physical therapy and limited mobility. It was a lot to endure for a teenager.

Why Wait?

Sometimes, we may wonder why we have to wait on God. Why can't he answer us immediately? What's the delay? For me (a teenager Amy), I asked questions like: why did I have to have this problem? Why didn't the brace work after enduring it for a year and a half? Why wasn't I healed by either prayer or professional doctors? Why did I have to be so obviously different from the other teens? It would have been so much easier if this had just gone away with the first prayer or even after enduring the brace. But it didn't.

Whether your suffering is physical, financial, psychological, or emotional, we all go through hard times. We do so as parents, and our kids do as well. At times we wonder where God is during those difficulties. It can be really hard to trust God in the midst of it, to trust that he's in control and that he will bring good out of the worst of things. Often life doesn't make sense, so it's hard to imagine that God cares.

Read John, chapter 9.

God Uses All Things

Some people assume that when you suffer or get sick, you are partially to blame. Maybe you did something bad and this is your punishment. Maybe your suffering is a physical manifestation of wrong thoughts or words.

Even Jesus' disciples were confused about why some suffer. They saw a blind man and assumed the blindness was a divine punishment for wrongs done:

> As he went along, he saw a man blind from birth. His disciples asked him, "Rabbi, who sinned, this man or his parents, that he was born blind?"
>
> "Neither this man nor his parents sinned," said Jesus, "but this happened so that the works of God might be displayed in him. (John 9:1-3 NIV)

Jesus made some mud and smeared it over his sightless eyes, then told him to go wash at the Pool of Siloam, a very public place. The man did and was suddenly able to see for the first time in his life. The miracle astonished his neighbors and caused enough of an uproar that the authorities investigated it.

While it certainly brought glory to God, we have no other explanation of why this man had to wait so many years for his miracle, yet when it did occur it was an obvious display of God's works since this was more than just a restoring of something lost, sick, or defective. The man had been born without sight, so this was something newly created.

Our Attempts to Explain Human Suffering

Even now, we unfortunately hear similar phrases among Christians, sayings like "you aren't healed because you don't have enough faith" or "you must be sinning and that's why you're suffering." Going through hard times is difficult enough, but when others blame us for our troubles it doubles the pain. We want sympathy and compassion, not condemnation or dismissal.

Sin does result in suffering, but not all suffering is caused by sin. We need to remember that for ourselves or we might think all bad things we encounter are somehow "our fault" when often they aren't. We also need to remind our kids of this truth, or else they may start blaming themselves for things that they didn't cause. We would love to spare our kids the pain of suffering, but we can't wrap them in bubble wrap and lock them away in a display case for safety. Our kids have their own lives to live, and that life will bring them its share of difficulties. It's our job as parents to help them acquire the skills to endure those times of suffering and come out of them even stronger spiritually.

Jesus knew that even his closest disciples would endure hardship. He took the time to warn them that is was coming and he also assured them, wanting them to have peace as they endured.

> "I have told you these things, so that in me you may have peace. In this world you will have trouble. But take heart! I have overcome the world." (John 16:33 NIV)

The truth of it is, God doesn't always tell us why we go through what we go through, but he does promise to be there for us as we go through it. That is the truth we should share with our kids. They need to know that there will be hard times, but they also need to know that God will always be there with them and will make something good out of even the worst of messes.

God's Timing for the World

When things get really bad, we might remind ourselves that all this will pass some day, that Jesus will return and redeem this world and rid it of all the wrongs. But then we might wonder why he hasn't returned already. The Apostle Peter answered that question almost two thousand years ago and his answer still holds:

> But do not forget this one thing, dear friends: With the Lord a day is like a thousand years, and a thousand years are like a day. The Lord is not slow in keeping his promise, as some understand slowness. Instead he is patient with you, not wanting anyone to perish, but everyone to come to repentance. (2 Peter 3:8-9 NIV)

Sometimes, the waiting is for a good reason. He pauses to allow one more person to embrace salvation before he brings it all to an end, and then one more, and another. Isn't it worth waiting for heaven if it allows more to join us?

Trusting Him

Jesus doesn't give us clearcut answers for everything we endure, and he certainly doesn't promise to rescue us from the difficulties and attacks. He even told us in advance that all of us Christians would endure persecution, but he also promises that his Holy Spirit will always be with us, no matter the circumstances. Finally, he also promises that all things (including the bad) will work together for good for those who trust him (Romans 8:28).

I (Amy) would have likely died if my scoliosis had gone untreated. I went through some very hard times as a young teen as my disorder worsened and then through the intense surgery to correct it. But the hardships I endured is what saved me and made me into the woman I am today.

All of us (including our kids) have gone through, are currently going through, or will go through times of suffering. That's life lived. We will *go through it*, but we have a choice: we can either let the suffering make us bitter, angry, fearful, distrusting, or resentful toward God, or we can allow the hard times to deepen our relationship with God and produce perseverance in us. We need to teach our kids that life is not about trying to avoid pain, but about trusting God even in the midst of it.

We can live with patience *and* purpose, knowing that God will see us through (whether it takes a day or a lifetime) and he will bring good out of it. We can learn to trust him even when we hurt and don't have the answers.

As parents, we need to remember that our kids are watching our reactions during the suffering. Hopefully, by watching us they will learn what it means to draw close to Jesus through the pain, developing their own testimony and their own story.

Daily Response

1. What are you or your kids going through right now? How has your response been?

2. How can you teach your kids to trust in God even when things aren't working out the way they hoped?

3. How can you as a family better support one another during times of trials?

Gathering ending Week 4
Notes

The Fruit of Kindness

But the fruit of the Spirit is love, joy, peace, forbearance, **kindness**, goodness, faithfulness, gentleness and self-control. Against such things there is no law. (Galatians 5:22-23 NIV *emphasis added*)

What is Kindness?

Kindness Will Cost

Amy: During my middle school years, there was a girl at my school who had Downs Syndrome who became the butt of endless jokes. I was a quiet 14-year-old, but I finally couldn't stay quiet about the abuse. One day during lunch, I confronted her worst abuser in front of a crowd, telling him to stop it. The bully became furious that I called him out in front of others. He did stop for a short time, but then that girl moved to a different school and the bully found a new target: me.

For weeks after that, he would call me names. Even during class, he would whisper profanities at me. Being kind and standing up for another cost me. Kindness usually does cost.

Pressure to be Unkind

How many times in our lives, have we been kind to another and it has cost us? The price we pay may be prestige, money, time, promotion, peace, social status, or even alienation of family or friends. The bullies will make us a target too, just because we resisted their bad behavior. In the worst situation, standing up for the other could even cost our life, as it has many reformers over the centuries.

Unfortunately, we live in a society that values the strong over the weak, the rich over the poor, the beautiful over the ordinary. It is hard to stand up to those messed-up standards because we fear what it will cost us. We don't want to be pushed aside ourselves and rejected too, whether that's on a school playground or in an office break room. We get scared, so we don't fight for the weak. We silently let it keep happening because we don't want to draw the bully's attention.

But our failing to stand up to injustice makes us unkind too.

Being a Good Samaritan

Jesus told a story that illustrates kindness in action. His story is so famous that millions use it as an example of what kindness to others looks like.

Read Luke 10:25-37

In the parable about loving even those who are strangers, Jesus tells about an unfortunate man who was attacked on a road that went through some very desolate terrain. The robbery was a rough one, leaving the man badly beaten and stripped of all valuables, including his clothes. He lay there on the side of the road, naked and half-dead. Jesus then tells of three different men who encountered the victim:

> A priest happened to be going down the same road, and when he saw the man, he passed by on the other side. So too, a Levite, when he came to the place and saw him, passed by on the other side. (Luke 10:31-32 NIV)

The two religious leaders chose to avoid the situation. We don't know for certain what motivated them to avoid the gravely injured man. Maybe they feared for their own lives, wondering if the robbers were still nearby. Maybe they didn't want to sully themselves by touching a bloody, filthy almost-corpse, convincing themselves that he would be dead soon anyway. Maybe they thought themselves too important to get involved, knowing that offering help would certainly delay their travels.

Both the priest and Levite didn't just walk past; they crossed over to the other side of the road to go around the mess. They probably looked away to avoid seeing too many details. They certainly made sure they were far enough away that if the man regained consciousness and tried to reach out, he wouldn't be able to touch them.

But then a third man came down the road, a man who was a despised foreigner. His reaction was very different- he actually stopped to help.

> He went to him and bandaged his wounds, pouring on oil and wine. Then he put the man on his own donkey, brought him to an inn and took care of him. The next day he took out two denarii and gave them to the innkeeper. 'Look after him,' he said, 'and when I return, I will reimburse you for any extra expense you may have.'
> (Luke 10:34-35 NIV)

The Samaritan not only gave first aid, he loaded the victim on his own transportation and then walked beside that donkey all the way to an inn. He got the man to safety but didn't stop helping. He got him a room for that night and then gave the innkeeper enough money to cover the man's room and care for another week or so, even promising to pay more if the expenses went any higher.

This foreigner proved that he was the true "neighbor" to the victim, because he was the one who showed mercy to a stranger. Then Jesus throws a real zinger at all of us when he says to "go and do likewise".

A Life of Kindness

Being kind is much more than saying nice things or being polite. Kindness is doing good for others. Kindness is standing against injustice. Kindness is charity. Kindness is honoring another human being. As Christians, we are called to walk the way of kindness. This isn't optional for us. As we allow God to guide us, kindness will be part of our life.

That bully who began attacking me (Amy) after I defended our classmate did eventually face the consequences. Once a teacher found out about his verbal abuse of me, we were all called into the principal's office and it was dealt with. But in life, not everything gets resolved that neatly. That fact shouldn't keep us from making kindness an essential part of who we are, but we need to realize that sometimes the bully or the "holier-than-thou" avoider gets away with their misdeeds. Our kids also need to learn that.

As parents, we are challenged to model and teach kindness to our children. For them to truly succeed in life, they need to learn this. As a little one, kindness might mean sharing a toy with another at preschool. As an elementary student, kindness might be befriending the new kid who seems lonely. As a teenager, kindness might be volunteering at a food pantry. We should help our children (whether they are toddlers or school-aged kids or young adults) to cultivate a lifestyle of kindness toward others.

Daily Response

1. Think about a time when you were kind to another. What did you do?

2. How can you be kind to your kid(s)?

3. How can you model kindness to your kid(s)?

Helping the Needy

Pandemic Poverty

Amy: When the COVID pandemic hit, I saw so much suffering in the community where I taught. In a matter of weeks, people went from living paycheck-to-paycheck to total destitution. So many worked at blue-collar jobs that couldn't be converted into work-from-home positions, so when the stores and warehouses closed, their incomes vanished. Those still working, suddenly faced having to decide whether it was safe to leave their kids home alone while they did their work shifts. It was a desperate time, even if they escaped getting ill.

The school I taught at had been running a food pantry for years, but even that shut down as fear and illness spread. So many of my students were suffering more than ever and I couldn't even talk to them in-person. We were on distance learning, so our only contact was over the Internet. It got so bad that the administration started asking for donations to help the neediest of families, which were so many.

Do We Notice?

Some of us have experienced extreme poverty and even homelessness. Eric had a friend in college whose father threw him out at 18, forcing the teen to live in his car for weeks until he scrounged enough money to rent a dilapidated trailer.

How many of us have seen a homeless person or known a friend who lost a job? The question is what do we do when we see it?

Being aware of poverty, whether we've experienced it ourselves or not, should move us to compassion.

Caring about the Needy

God cares about the poor among us and he want to bless them through us, the people who encounter them:

> Whoever oppresses the poor shows contempt for their Maker, but
> whoever is kind to the needy honors God. (Proverbs 14:31 NIV)

Sometimes, we can become cynical toward those begging for money on street corners, on highway off-ramps, at gas stations, and in front of stores. We wonder how many of them are really in need. We wonder if they are going to use the money for a tank of gas or for drugs. We become hardened and even fearful of these often-dirty strangers, so we don't make eye contact as we pass them. If we encounter too many, we might even start complaining or calling for their removal from our area. It is an understandable reaction- Eric and I have felt that discomfort ourselves- but it isn't what God calls for us to do. In the above passage, God calls us to be kind to the poor, and in so doing we honor God who made that person.

We need to be careful, because if we hold an attitude of uncaring we could become oppressive, and that is showing contempt toward God. Kicking a bum is like kicking God. Spitting or mocking a poor person is like doing the same to our Lord, according to Proverbs. But on the positive side, when we are kind to them we also honor God.

> Whoever is kind to the poor lends to the Lord, and he will reward them
> for what they have done. (Proverbs 19:17 NIV)

It is amazing that we can honor God by helping the poor and that God considers anything we give to the poor as his own debt that he will repay. As a wise man once said, "We give, so that we can get (from God), so that we can give even more."

Charity to the needy can be done individually and it can be done by a whole congregation. In the early years of Christianity, some of the churches raised money to help other congregations that were struggling through a drought and other crises. Paul told the believers in Corinth about some of those giving congregations:

> And now, brothers and sisters, we want you to know about the grace
> that God has given the Macedonian churches. In the midst of a very severe
> trial, their overflowing joy and their extreme poverty welled up in rich
> generosity. For I testify that they gave as much as they were able, and even
> beyond their ability. Entirely on their own, they urgently pleaded with us
> for the privilege of sharing in this service to the Lord's people. And they
> exceeded our expectations: They gave themselves first of all to the Lord,
> and then by the will of God also to us.
> (2 Corinthians 8:1-5 NIV)

Practical Help

Please note, God is not calling on us to give into every whim or demand of the poor. Even if we give away all that we have, there would still be an overwhelming amount of poor people in this world. He's not asking us to solve the world's poverty; he's telling us to respect the poor we do encounter. Treat them with dignity and help them as we can.

Sometimes that help will be a donation to a fundraiser or sponsoring a child overseas every month. Sometimes it might mean helping out every week at a food pantry or maybe giving a few dollars to a beggar we'll likely never see again.

Such help is especially vital when it's our fellow Christian who is in need. Even though the believers in Macedonia were struggling themselves, they still found a way to give generously to another church that was facing an even worse situation. Believers helping other believers.

Daily Response

1. Think back over your Christian life. What are some of the things you've done to help the needy?

2. Have you ever failed to model "helping the needy" to your child? How could you model that better to them?

3. What are some practical things you and your child could do together to help the poor?

Respect and Fairness

Not Good Enough for Church

Eric: When I was a young Christian, the California church I attended had an outreach program to reach folks that had attended a Sunday service and had filled out a visitation card. I decided to volunteer, even though I'm not the most outgoing of guys. What the group did was connect with everyone who filled out one of those cards. We would visit their homes, give them some more information about the church, pray with them if they wanted, and then we would invite them to come back next Sunday. We usually went out in pairs, which meant I was often matched up with one of the other single guys.

One of the guys I got to know was a nice fellow the exact same age as me, but some of the leaders didn't like having him volunteer. It wasn't his personality- he had a much friendlier disposition than I did. The problem was that he was a good 'ol boy, a rather large fellow who spoke with a strong Southern drawl and dressed like he was right off the farm. He was an upright young man, friendly and welcoming, but he was too much of a country bumpkin. It wasn't the image some of the leaders wanted portrayed about "our church". They certainly didn't respect this brother-in-Christ, but instead found him to be an embarrassment to them.

Sadly, the leaders convinced him to stop volunteering. Unfortunately, I didn't stand up for him either, which I regret to this day. He deserved better treatment from his Christian brethren.

All About Image

Maybe this isn't a temptation for you, but many of us can get caught up on how we (or our kids) look and who's in our circle of friends. Like those church leaders mentioned above, we might even lose respect for those who don't fit our preferred image. We can become unkind, even judgmental.

Have you ever experienced someone making a snap decision about you? Maybe it was at a business meeting, at a dinner gathering, at a kid's birthday party, or at a friend's barbecue.

You've just met this person and you can tell they've already dismissed you as unimportant. They aren't even interested in small talk, instead they are already looking elsewhere. You are a nobody to them, and that can be a hurtful experience.

When our kids are judged it can be even more upsetting. We know that our kids are great and talented and smart in their own way, but then others dismiss them as not good enough.

Sadly, this kind of dismissal of us or our kids can even happen among Christians.

Playing Favorites in Church

In a letter to the Jewish believers of his day, James collected his best teachings and instructions to help them with everyday life as a Christian. Included in his wise words is a section about favoritism during church gatherings:

> My brothers and sisters, believers in our glorious Lord Jesus Christ must not show favoritism. Suppose a man comes into your meeting wearing a gold ring and fine clothes, and a poor man in filthy old clothes also comes in. If you show special attention to the man wearing fine clothes and say, "Here's a good seat for you," but say to the poor man, "You stand there" or "Sit on the floor by my feet," have you not discriminated among yourselves and become judges with evil thoughts?
>
> Listen, my dear brothers and sisters: Has not God chosen those who are poor in the eyes of the world to be rich in faith and to inherit the kingdom he promised those who love him? But you have dishonored the poor. Is it not the rich who are exploiting you? Are they not the ones who are dragging you into court? Are they not the ones who are blaspheming the noble name of him to whom you belong? (James 2:1-7 NIV)

It might be surprising to read what James was confronting. Sometimes we think the early church was so much more noble than we are now, but they also faced temptations like playing favorites, which is a lure to all groups whether it be a small group or a large church assembly. And just like James faced, it is a sin that is all too easily tolerated. This isn't a hidden sin; it is often done out in the open. The church James confronted was giving special treatment to the rich-and-famous, blatantly giving them the best seats. They were also openly snubbing the shabby poor, telling them to get out of the way. This still happens today and folks are proud of it. Just a few days ago I (Eric) read an article interviewing the pastor of a very popular church that had a private entrance and roped-off premium seating for the famous who attended so that the riffraff wouldn't bother them. The pastor was proud about his church's sin. It was like they were saying that if you aren't a "star" you are a second-rate

Christian; go sit in the back and just be happy that you can be in the same room as these far-more-important Christians.

Who are Your Favorites?

It might be easy for us to see the sin of a church that caters to the rich-and-famous, but all of us can face similar temptations to play favorites, even among our fellow believers. We stay around people who we feel comfortable around, avoiding those who are "different", whether that is because of age, ethnicity, status, occupation, or any of a hundred other reasons. We will be tempted to judge people by how they look, talk, or dress rather than by their character and commitment to Christ.

There's nothing wrong with enjoying certain people's company more than others. We all have our preferences and dislikes. I enjoy epic fantasy stories more than zombie tales. Amy drinks coffee while I avoid the stuff. I have a friend who regularly runs for exercise, while I only run because of imminent danger. Spending more time with those who have a lot in common with us isn't wrong. The sin isn't liking someone more than another; the sin is being dismissive or unkind. The sin is being unfair and disrespectful to the "others." It is even worse if we teach our kids to do the same.

Our kids will have their best friends and then others who they can't relate to as well. That is true for all of us. There is no need for them to feel guilty about preferring to spend time with certain people over others, but they still need to treat every fellow human with respect and fairness. As long as they've learned that, we've done well as parents.

Daily Response

1. Have you ever been overlooked because you weren't the favorite? How did that feel?

2. Why is favoritism wrong?

3. How can you model being fair to your children?

4. How can you teach your children to avoid the sin of favoritism?

Blessing with our Spiritual Gifts

Spirit led?

Eric: When I finally went to college, I was about ten years older than most others. It was natural for some of the students to look to me for advice since I was the "old man" on campus, and at times God would gift me with words of wise counsel. But sometimes I was more filled with manure than Spirit while talking with my younger friends. God gave me an embarrassing teaching moment one late afternoon that I still remember.

A group of us were sitting in the college cafeteria/ lounge area and I had just bloviated about something, rambling off some inane advice until God caught me. Suddenly convicted, I stopped giving *my advice* and told the others to ignore everything I had just said because it was useless hot air rather than any words of wisdom. It was kind of an embarrassing thing to admit, but at least it was with friends.

A bit later, as evening was settling in, we split up to head home. In the parking lot, a few of us encountered some other classmates, one of whom sought me out for advice right there among the rows of cars. Without really being aware of it, I was able to offer them some godly advice that was gladly received.

After sharing, I suddenly realized what God had done. Shaking my head and chuckling, I could only thank him. He had shown me the difference between "words of Eric" and "words of wisdom," and that only the later could be a blessing to others.

God taught me the importance of giving to others what He has given me, rather than just giving others something that I've generated on my own.

As Close as the Holy Spirit

Depending on our past experiences, we might think of God as rather aloof- he seems far away and not really that concerned with our life. However, whenever we think that we are actually making a mistake. He has placed his Holy Spirit inside of each of us- we can't get much closer than that. He is here to guide us to truth, assure us of our salvation, and to empower us for doing good.

One of the sweet things that the Holy Spirit does is that he gifts us with abilities we wouldn't naturally have so that we can make a God-glorifying difference in the lives of others. His presents to us aren't for us to horde or hide or hinder. His presents are meant to be used for the betterment of our fellow believers and the unsaved.

Have you ever seen your kids try to use a present without taking the time to read the instructions? Frustration or failure likely occurred, as they assembled it incorrectly and maybe even broke it. Similarly, we cannot use any spiritual gifts properly without direction of the Holy Spirit who dwells in us. We need to be sensitive to his guidance.

Give It Away

God gives us spiritual gifts so that we can bless others. They aren't meant for our entertainment or as something to boast about. In Acts, we read about Peter giving health to a lame man, something the man had never had before.

> One day Peter and John were going up to the temple at the time of prayer—at three in the afternoon. Now a man who was lame from birth was being carried to the temple gate called Beautiful, where he was put every day to beg from those going into the temple courts. When he saw Peter and John about to enter, he asked them for money. Peter looked straight at him, as did John. Then Peter said, "Look at us!" So the man gave them his attention, expecting to get something from them.
>
> Then Peter said, "Silver or gold I do not have, but what I do have I give you. In the name of Jesus Christ of Nazareth, walk." Taking him by the right hand, he helped him up, and instantly the man's feet and ankles became strong. He jumped to his feet and began to walk. Then he went with them into the temple courts, walking and jumping, and praising God. When all the people saw him walking and praising God, they recognized him as the same man who used to sit begging at the temple gate called Beautiful, and they were filled with wonder and amazement at what had happened to him.
>
> (Acts 3:1-10 NIV)

Peter freely shared what God had given him to share, which was healing in the powerful name of Jesus. That man wasn't expecting it- he had never known anything except the inability to walk. It was a great kindness to heal him, releasing him from a life of begging. It was also a kindness to the friends and family who had been carrying him to his begging spot every day. Spiritual gifts well applied are like that- they show God's kindness to others.

Supernatural

The New Testament offers multiple lists and examples of spiritual gifts, so we won't try to list them here. We would encourage you to study those passages if you want to learn more, like Romans 12, 1 Corinthians 12-14, Ephesians 4, and 1 Peter 4. One thing Amy and I have found, is that God's gifts are a way for us to show others that God sees them and wants to be involved in their life.

God really doesn't need us. He could intervene in people's lives without working through us. He could proclaim his Good News through angels or rocks; he doesn't need to share his truth with the lost through messed-up messengers like us. But God wants to do this. He wants us intimately involved in bringing others to salvation, to truth, to healing, to peace. He often does his supernatural acts through us so that we can experience it and be encouraged and amazed too.

God also wants to work through our children, no matter their age. He wants them as his messengers of hope. If our children are saved, then he has already gifted them with spiritual gifts. Their particular gifting might not be obvious to us, especially if they are still very young, but it will become clearer as we encourage them to follow Jesus daily.

Daily Response

1. How do you think spiritual gifts can show kindness to others?

2. What spiritual gifts have you experienced in your life?

3. How can you encourage your children to discover their spiritual gifts?

Considerate of Others

Just Make a Decision!

Amy: When Eric's eldest brother died, I wanted to solve the immediate problem: the funeral was going to be over a thousand miles away and we needed to get there. So I pushed Eric to make a decision: do we fly or drive? Could we afford all three of us going? (Our eldest was just a toddler at that time.) I was so concerned about the logistics that I wasn't considerate of Eric's distress. Although he hadn't been very close to his oldest brother since there was a twenty-two year age gap between them, this was still his sibling. I pushed for an immediate decision because I wanted it settled, but I wasn't noticing how hard my husband was taking his loss. It escalated into one of the few yelling fights we've ever had, and that ended with Eric slamming the back door so hard that it broke the blinds on the window.

Frustration with our Kids

We can all experience frustration with others, and in our frustration we can become inconsiderate. We can become unkind. It can happen in marriage, among friends, and at work. Sadly, it can also happen with our kids. Sometimes we forget how young they are and become frustrated with their immaturity and youthfulness.

For most of us, parenting is a 24/7 responsibility and it's for life. We can switch jobs if our current one isn't to our liking, but we can't switch families. We're stuck with them and they're stuck with us, especially our kids. Our children have us as parents and as role models. They learn a lot from us, especially during those stressful moments and how we handle our frustrations.

Are we modeling for our kids how to be considerate toward others, even when things aren't going the way we want? Are they learning how to be kind toward others all the time, and not just when they are getting their way?

Young, Single, and In Charge

The Apostle Paul had a handful of young men that he considered his *spiritual sons*. He had them join him as he followed Jesus, discipled them into leadership, and then eventually gave them their own responsibilities. Timothy was one of those sons who went on to pastor a church as a young and single guy. In the Bible we have two letters Paul wrote to him, full of words of warning, encouragement, and instructions, including the passage below:

> Flee the evil desires of youth and pursue righteousness, faith, love and peace, along with those who call on the Lord out of a pure heart. Don't have anything to do with foolish and stupid arguments, because you know they produce quarrels. And the Lord's servant must not be quarrelsome but must be kind to everyone, able to teach, not resentful. Opponents must be gently instructed, in the hope that God will grant them repentance leading them to a knowledge of the truth, and that they will come to their senses and escape from the trap of the devil, who has taken them captive to do his will. (2 Timothy 2:22-26 NIV)

Paul wants Timothy to set an example to the rest of the congregation, even though he's probably younger than many of them. He's to avoid lust and stupid arguments (there are always people who want to argue about something), to be kind to everyone (not just those who are friends or supporters), and to gently instruct any opponents in the hope that they will repent from their errors.

He's instructing Timothy to be a considerate leader rather than one who lords it over everyone. The aim is a congregation of people who are kind to each other, willing to learn (and teach), and aren't resentful. Most of us would probably love to be involved in a church like that.

Teaching Kindness and Consideration

We can learn from Paul and how he instructed his spiritual son. Maybe our kids aren't young adults like Timothy, but we can still start now in teaching them to be "kind to everyone".

The society around us seems to enjoy arguing, sarcastic attacks, and holding on to resentments, but we and our children are meant to be different. We are called to show kindness and to be considerate of others. We are even to take the time and effort to gently instruct our opponents, in the hope they will gain repentance before God. If we and our kids do these things, it will be noticed. We might be mocked for seeming to be gullible or naive, but we will certainly be different in our behavior.

Daily Response

1. Can you remember a time when you **succeeded** or **failed** being considerate in front of your kids?

2. How can you *model* to your child to be considerate of others?

3. How can you *teach* your child to be considerate of others?

Gathering ending Week 5
Notes

The Fruit of Goodness

But the fruit of the Spirit is love, joy, peace, forbearance, kindness, **goodness**, faithfulness, gentleness and self-control. Against such things there is no law. (Galatians 5:22-23 NIV *emphasis added*)

What is Goodness?

Life of Crime

Amy: At the age of four I would go to a babysitter after preschool, along with numerous other little ones. One day, I was tempted by a shiny trinket. It was just lying there, discarded by one of the other kids. When the babysitter asked who it belonged to, I claimed it was mine and greedily pocketed it. I wasn't quite muttering "my Precious" like Gollum in *The Lord of Rings*, but I was glad to have it in my possession.

I kept it hidden when my mom picked me up, keeping my trinket safely concealed in my pocket. It wasn't until later that evening that I finally felt convicted of my crime. In tears, I confessed to my parents about the stolen goody. The next day, I had to return it to my babysitter (to get it back to its rightful owner) and apologize for my actions. My early life of crime ended then, thankfully without any jail time.

Good vs. Bad

When something is good, we usually want to celebrate it and let everyone know. Look at this good! But when we've done something wrong, we are more likely to hide and deceive, like I did with that trinket.

Instinctively, we know the difference between good and bad, right and wrong. The Holy Spirit convicts of such, even as a preschooler. But as we grow older, our understanding of what is truly good can get muddied. It gets muddied by us justifying our own desires. It gets muddied by our failed expectations and disappointments in life. We can start questioning what is really good.

Sadly, many decide that what is "good" is whatever brings them pleasure or satisfaction. And many decide that "good" is dependent on the circumstances. God is good when life is going great, but God is bad if things aren't going our way. To combat such fallacies, we need to learn what goodness really is.

Who is Good?

Jesus once brought up the issue of who is good, when a rich young man came up to him with a question about eternal life.

> As Jesus started on his way, a man ran up to him and fell on his knees before him. "Good teacher," he asked, "what must I do to inherit eternal life?"
>
> "Why do you call me good?" Jesus answered. "No one is good—except God alone. You know the commandments: 'You shall not murder, you shall not commit adultery, you shall not steal, you shall not give false testimony, you shall not defraud, honor your father and mother.'" (Mark 10: 17-19 NIV)

Please notice that Jesus isn't forbidding the guy from calling him "good." He just wants to make sure the fellow understands what he's saying about Jesus by calling him good, that only God is good. The young man decided he wasn't ready to admit Jesus' divinity, so in the next verse he just calls him "teacher" and not "good teacher".

I think most of us are fine with admitting Jesus' divinity and would be quick to call him good, but that leads to another question. How can we cultivate the spiritual fruit of goodness in us and our children when only God is good? How do we reconcile those two?

How Can We Be Good?
Read Ephesians chapter 2:1-10

> For it is by grace you have been saved, through faith—and this is not from yourselves, it is the gift of God— not by works, so that no one can boast. For we are God's handiwork, created in Christ Jesus to do good works, which God prepared in advance for us to do. (Ephesians 2:8-10 NIV)

We can do good because God made us and intended us to do so in Christ Jesus. We aren't good out of our own doing; we are good because he has crafted us that way, as a new creation upon our salvation. So the goodness isn't innate- it isn't a natural part of us. The goodness in us is from his presence in us, his handiwork as he turns us into a new person in Christ.

He does the same with each of our children as they come to repentance and salvation.

Remade in Jesus

We can only be good because of what he has done *for* us and *in* us. First, what he has done **for** us: he took our sins upon himself and made it possible for us to be reconciled with Father God. He gifted us with salvation. Second, what he has done **in** us: his Holy Spirit has come to indwell each of us upon our salvation and he never leaves. He is there to comfort us, to guide us, to empower us for service, and to provide us answers.

For our children, it's the same way. No matter how sweet or intelligent they are, they need the salvation of Jesus to ever be "good". When as parents we ignore our kids' sinfulness, we do them a disservice. Kids need Jesus as much as their parents do.

Once we are saved, once we've become a child of God, then and only then can we start cultivating true goodness in our life.

Daily Response

1. Is Jesus your savior? (If not, then it is time to consider letting go of your sin, your wrongs, and accepting his offer to pay for you wrongs with his own life.) Do your children know Jesus as their savior?

2. How is the Holy Spirit working in your life this week? How has he brought out goodness in you?

3. What could you do this week to encourage your kids to cultivate goodness in their life?

Help or Hinder?

God is Watching!

Eric: There's a story told of a crotchety Sunday School teacher who was getting frustrated with a rowdy group of kids, especially with one particular boy who was full of energy and apparently incapable of sitting still. Tired of one disruption after another, the teacher finally tried pulling the *God card* to get them to behave.

"You better start behaving! God is watching you right now. Do you want God mad at you? He's always watching you!" the teacher threatened.

The words hit the rowdiest boy hard. He swallowed in sudden fear, imagining God glaring down from high overhead.

Afterward, when his mom asked him how Sunday School was, he muttered something incoherent. She could tell something was upsetting him, but he wouldn't say anything more.

Finally, when they pulled up at their home, he blurted out the question that had been eating him up inside. "Does God really watch me all the time?"

His mother knew her son and that he was used to adults keeping an eye on him because of his boisterous personality, ready to call him out for the slightest misstep. *Watching adults* usually meant that they were noticing something they didn't like and some kind of punishment was on its way. She didn't want her son thinking that God was like those sour adults.

With sudden insight, she smiled and answered, "Of course God watches you. He loves you so much that he can't take his eyes off you. God loves watching you."

Her son's face suddenly brightened. "Really? He must think I'm special."

Mom nodded, "Oh yes, you are very important to him and he loves you greatly."

What that Sunday School teacher had done was misrepresent God. The teacher implied that God would be sitting in angry judgment of those rowdy kids, giving the children a warped picture of their heavenly Father.

In Numbers 20:1-13 we read that Moses did something similar, when he got angry at the Israelites during their time in the desert. They had been upset about the lack of water, bemoaning the wasteland that Moses had led them into and longing for the place they had left behind, and Moses got sick of it. God told Moses to gather the people and "speak to that rock before their eyes and it will pour out its water." (v. 8) In his anger, Moses started hitting the rock with his staff instead of just speaking to it, letting all his frustration show. God graciously still gave them water, but later Moses faced the consequences for misrepresenting God to his people.

Representing God

As parents, we can sometimes misrepresent God to our kids too. They watch what we do and how we act, and they will think that God must be just like us, with our flaws and issues. Although we will never be perfect parents (at least Amy and I will never be that), we can do things that will help our kids realize that the Lord values them and that he certainly does watch them nonstop out of his great love for them.

They have the Kingdom

Too often, our society belittles or ignores children. They are seen as pests that will interrupt dinner plans with their loudness or will surely spread germs with their sticky hands. Kids aren't important or influential. Getting to know a kid isn't going to advance your career. Kids aren't the "movers and shakers" of society. For many, children should be well-behaved and kept from getting underfoot.

Jesus' disciples saw them as an interruption too and tried to keep the little kids away, but Jesus stopped them.

> People were bringing little children to Jesus for him to place his hands on them, but the disciples rebuked them. When Jesus saw this, he was indignant. He said to them, "Let the little children come to me, and do not hinder them, for the kingdom of God belongs to such as these. Truly I tell you, anyone who will not receive the kingdom of God like a little child will never enter it." And he took the children in his arms, placed his hands on them and blessed them. (Mark 10:13-16 NIV)

The disciples thought of themselves as the insiders, as the guys with a close connection to God. Jesus shattered those thoughts when he told them the kingdom belonged to those like the children they tried to exclude. He told them they couldn't even enter the kingdom unless they received it like a little kid.

Modeling God Truthfully

As adults, we can grow impatient with children and even want to exclude them from things because they are too much of a distraction, especially if they aren't our children. But when it comes to spiritual things, we should be as kid-friendly as possible because our attitude will color their ideas of what God is like. If we are welcoming, then they will likely think God is welcoming too. If we lose our temper like that Sunday School teacher or like Moses, then they will likely think that God is easily angered. If we push them away like the disciples tried, then kids are likely to think that God doesn't want anything to do with them.

Whether we like it or not, we have great influence on the children around us. How we model God to them will likely stay with them for the rest of their lives. We want to model God to others in a truthful way; we don't want them to get the wrong picture of him.

Daily Response

1. Think about your own childhood. What people and events shaped your idea of who God is?

2. As an adult Christian, what has influenced your view of God?

3. How can you help your kid(s) to get closer to Jesus?

Walking in Wisdom

Sharing What I Know

Eric: Last year there was a Fall day when the weather changed, becoming noticeably cooler. When I started the car that morning a warning light came on: low tire pressure. Using it as a teaching moment, I had one of my sons help to check and refill the air. I showed him where to find the recommended pressure listed on the door jamb and on the tire. I showed him how to plug in the tire inflator and how to attach it to the tire's valve stem.

Here are a few other practical lessons that I've shared with my children:

- "Wash your hands after using the toilet."
- "Righty tighty; lefty loosey."
- "Preheat the oven to 350F."

I'm full of little bits of advice, from how to change a furnace filter to the right way to make an omelet. I want to pass on as much practical knowledge as I can to my kids. It's something that I learned from my mother, who made sure that I (her youngest son) knew the basics of cooking, sewing, and checkbook balancing before I went out to live on my own.

Like almost all parents, I want to give my kids lots of practical advice that will help them survive when they grow up and move away.

What are you Teaching your Kids?

In Proverbs chapter 3, we encounter a father teaching his son, but these lessons are much bigger than "how to check your car's tire pressure." This dad is confident that his lessons (if applied for life) will do some wondrous things:

- Prolong his son's life
- Bring his son peace
- Bring his son prosperity

Reading that, I want to ditch all those other little lessons. Dang! I want to teach my kids' the kind of stuff that the Proverbs dad is teaching! Clean hands are good, but a longer life is much better. Knowing how to do minor home repairs is important, but finding peace and prosperity is at a whole different level. I need to step up my game; I needed to be teaching on far more important stuff than I have been.

On reading this passage in Proverbs, I realized the possibility of having other teaching priorities that could be far more advantageous to my kids. Here's how that dad introduces what he's about to teach:

> My son, do not forget my teaching, but keep my commands in your heart, for they will prolong your life many years and bring you peace and prosperity. (Proverbs 3:1-2 NIV)

He's promising quite a bit to his kid. So let's look at what he thinks is so vital and life-changing.

Walk in Wisdom

Read Proverbs 3

This dad isn't teaching his son how to plow a field, launder his clothes, cook a good stew, or to sharpen a knife. Those are all practical skills that he might have taught him as well, but the focus here is on the goodness of his character. He teaches him to:

1. **Make love and faithfulness a lifelong priority** (v. 3), which in turn results in "Then you will win favor and a good name in the sight of God and man." (Proverbs 3:4 NIV) When we or our children are consistently caring and trustworthy, we get a reputation as such.

2. **Trust God completely, submitting to him** (v. 5-6) rather than doing things by what you judge is best.

3. **Fear God and shun evil**, rather than relying on your own smarts. (v. 7) We need a healthy fear and respect of our great God. Out of that respect, we ought to totally reject evil rather than flirting with wrongness or thinking that some bad behavior is funny or justified.

4. **Honor God with your wealth and increase.** (v. 9) We honor God by using our income/ wealth for good (as opposed to selfish reasons), by giving to support fellow Christians in ministry, and by sharing what we have with those who are in need. Our kids also need to learn to honor God with their finances.

5. **Don't despise God's discipline.** (v. 11) God cares so much for us that he will intervene and correct us when we aren't doing right. We shouldn't hate his correction or curse that it happened- he did this to get our attention so that we will realize our need to admit our wrong and do better. We should teach our kids to have that same attitude towards God's discipline- it's not an easy thing to learn but

it is so vital for us.

In verses 13-20, the dad talks about Wisdom as if it is a woman and as if Understanding is her sister. Where most young guys will be focused on pursuing the prettiest woman they can find, he's encouraging his son to pursue Wisdom with that same kind of intensity and purpose.

In verses 21-26, he promises his son some great blessings if he will diligently chase after wisdom, from restful sleep to protection from the disasters that wipe out the foolish. By embracing wisdom, he will have a clear conscience and be able to avoid those snares in life that will catch others in awful sin. For our kids to have a long and prosperous life, they will need to pursue wisdom too.

In verses 27- 31, the Proverbs dad gives a list of "Do Nots" that will make any kid into a great member of society, one who treats others fairly and avoids evil.

Finally, in verses 32-35, the dad shows that God isn't aloof. God takes sides, working against the evil, the proud mockers, and the fools. His implied question to his son: do you want to be on God's side or not?

Being Purposeful in Teaching our Kids

When it comes to preparing our kids for adulthood, we can miss the bigger lessons. We can forget to take the time to actually teach them what it means to be a person of good character. They will hopefully learn a lot from seeing us model wise behavior but, like the Proverbs dad, we need to take the time to actually talk to our kids about pursuing wisdom.

If we want our children to have peace and prosperity, we need to teach them God's truth like this dad did.

Daily Response

1. How can you make love and faithfulness a priority in your life? How can you teach your kids to do the same?

2. What does it mean to trust and submit to God? How can you show your kids how to do this?

3. What does it mean to fear God? Does it mean to be scared of God?

4. How can you honor God with your income/ wealth? How can you teach your kids to honor God that way too?

5. Has God ever disciplined you? What was that like?

Imitate Jesus (and Others)

Copycat

Amy: When I was five, I had the vocabulary of an eight-year-old. However, when my dad went with me to a kindergarten function, he was shocked at how my vocabulary suddenly regressed to that of a barely-talking preschooler. He was confused and upset at his little girl's strange setback. It took a bit of time for my parents to realize what I was doing: I was imitating my friends in the class that weren't as advanced as I was. Little me was trying to fit in by imitating their babyish talk. My parents were not amused.

I experienced similar copycat behavior with my own kids many years later. When our boys were younger, they sometimes wanted to "dress like Daddy", which was always cute to see. They wore button shirts with t-shirts underneath, just like Dad. They would try to wear his much-too-big shoes as well. Eric and I would smile at their copying ways.

Kids like to imitate, whether it's their friends, parents, or favorite hero. Sometimes they pick someone decent to copy, and sometimes they make a lousy choice.

Who Influences Us?

In some ways, we never outgrow that desire to be like someone else. We admire their bravery, success, looks, or influence. It's one of the reasons that manufacturers pay huge amounts of money to get celebrity endorsements of their products, because we want that thing that our favorite superstar is selling, be it a drink, a car, or a walk-in tub for the aged.

Advertisers also work hard to reach our kids, wanting to win them as a loyal lifetime fan. They use guilt, envy, lust, greed, shame, or anything else that will hook our kids. They sneak their product into movies, song lyrics, and video games. Frankly, the advertisers want to have a greater influence over of our kids than we do.

Typically, we (and our children) are influenced by someone, somehow and in some way. It might be someone we know well, like a parent or mentor or a good friend. It might be someone we admire from afar, like a celebrity or an historic figure or even a fictional character. As a Christian, we should be more purposeful at who we are choosing to imitate.

Who do We Imitate?

Wanting to model ourselves after someone else can be a good thing, but only if we have the right person to copy. We aren't just talking about imitating another's fashion sense, health habits, cooking technique, or investment strategy. The Bible is encouraging us to imitate others when it comes to our approach to life. The Apostle Paul even points to himself as a role model, at least to those who knew him as a spiritual dad:

> I am writing this not to shame you but to warn you as my dear children. Even if you had ten thousand guardians in Christ, you do not have many fathers, for in Christ Jesus I became your father through the gospel. Therefore I urge you to imitate me. For this reason I have sent to you Timothy, my son whom I love, who is faithful in the Lord. He will remind you of my way of life in Christ Jesus, which agrees with what I teach everywhere in every church (1 Corinthians 4:14-17 NIV)

Paul wants them to imitate him, to copy his "way of life in Christ Jesus." It wasn't just the believers in Corinth who were looking to him as a role model. Those in the city of Thessaloníki had done the same:

> You became imitators of us and of the Lord, for you welcomed the message in the midst of severe suffering with the joy given by the Holy Spirit. And so you became a model to all the believers in Macedonia and Achaia. (1 Thessalonians 1:6-7 NIV)

Paul states that these believers imitated both him and Jesus, and that they became a role model to others.

WWJD?

In 1896 the novel *In His Steps* posed the question "What Would Jesus Do?", influencing many Christians to become more socially active and make a difference in their community. One hundred years later, in the 1990s, the WWJD bracelets became a huge fad among Christian youth groups, as once again believers asked how Jesus would face life's situations.

The book is still a decent read (although it shows its age) and wearing a rubber bracelet can still offer a visual reminder to ask an important question of ourselves, but neither book nor bracelet is necessary to get this message across to our kids. We (Amy and Eric) think the best way to encourage kids to model their lives after Jesus is to help them really get to know him. They need to hear and read what Jesus said and did. They need to learn to speak to him and listen for his reply. They need to see how he has changed others. When our kids get to know Jesus, they will definitely realize he is worth imitating.

Daily Response

1. Who have you imitated in your life? Have you had any mentors or heroes that you've tried to copy?

2. Who do your children look up to? Who are their heroes or role models?

3. How can you help your kids look toward Jesus as someone to imitate?

Power of Your Tongue

Lies for Laughs

Eric: It's a popular ice-breaker to help a group relax, get to know each other, and have some fun. Most of you reading this book have probably played it before at some gathering somewhere. It's called Two Truths and a Lie, and I despise it. In the game, each player tells two facts about themselves and one falsehood, then everyone else tries to guess which one of the three statements is the lie. You hear all kinds of wild stories, as people reveal where they've traveled, mishaps that they've experienced, and adventures they've had. It can be a great way to learn some trivia about the others in the room, but it is a game that I avoid whenever I can.

I hate the game because I could be a great liar if I wanted. I'm a storyteller who writes novels, so I have a great imagination. All that I need to add is a straight face and I can tell you all sorts of whoppers that seem true. That skill is something far too dangerous for me to be playing with. I don't need a group a people enjoying my deceptions- that would encourage me to mislead elsewhere, which is something I've done before.

Don't misunderstand me- I wasn't a chronic liar as a kid, but I was a word manipulator. As a teen, before I became a Christ follower, I was known for my sarcastic barbs, joking exaggerations, and my ability to say the most innocent thing at *just the right moment* and in *just the right tone* to make it obscene. I didn't cuss; I just twisted words to my own foul ends. I hurt more than a few friends with my biting "jokes", which is something I still regret. I never physically beat up anybody, but my words left far too many bruises.

That's why I have no desire to get good at misleading with my words. No thanks. I've done enough damage with sarcasm and off-color innuendos. Why would I want to arm my tongue with another hurtful skill?

Words that Wound or Heal

We live in a society that often celebrates lying and verbal deception. Breaking your word or hurting others with your words isn't seen as so awful, because the "sticks and stones may break my bones, but words can never hurt me" syndrome. We think words don't matter that much, but they really do. The words we heard as children, both positive and negative, both truthful and deceptive, had an impact on the adult we became. The words we say around and over our own children will be with them for the rest of their lives.

Words count, so what kind of words should we be saying?

Words Matter

James, the brother of Jesus, wrote about how hard it is to control your words:

> Not many of you should become teachers, my fellow believers, because you know that we who teach will be judged more strictly. We all stumble in many ways. Anyone who is never at fault in what they say is perfect, able to keep their whole body in check.
>
> When we put bits into the mouths of horses to make them obey us, we can turn the whole animal. Or take ships as an example. Although they are so large and are driven by strong winds, they are steered by a very small rudder wherever the pilot wants to go. Likewise, the tongue is a small part of the body, but it makes great boasts. Consider what a great forest is set on fire by a small spark. The tongue also is a fire, a world of evil among the parts of the body. It corrupts the whole body, sets the whole course of one's life on fire, and is itself set on fire by hell.
>
> All kinds of animals, birds, reptiles and sea creatures are being tamed and have been tamed by mankind, but no human being can tame the tongue. It is a restless evil, full of deadly poison.
>
> With the tongue we praise our Lord and Father, and with it we curse human beings, who have been made in God's likeness. Out of the same mouth come praise and cursing. My brothers and sisters, this should not be. Can both fresh water and salt water flow from the same spring? My brothers and sisters, can a fig tree bear olives, or a grapevine bear figs? Neither can a salt spring produce fresh water. (James 3:1-12 NIV)

Taming Our Tongues

When I became a Christian, I had to work hard to break the habits of sarcasm, exaggeration, and crude innuendos. It took years to learn to use a more corny, self-deprecating humor. Retraining my tongue wasn't easy, but it was worth it. I'm a kinder man now. My words aren't tempting, deceiving, or hurting others. Do I have perfect word-control? Of course not, but the change has been a good one nonetheless.

As James says above, our little tongue has so much power, so retraining that tongue isn't easy. We may have the habit of using our words to flirt, attack, mislead, put down, control, harass, tempt, berate, lie, gossip, belittle, confuse, deceive, undermine, or hurt. Any of those habits would be difficult to break, yet clearing out as many as possible is very much worth it. We need to learn tongue-control- to learn how to tame our wild words so that they no longer damage others or defame God.

We also have a responsibility to model and teach our children to speak with clarity, honesty, care, empathy, and goodness. We aren't talking about suppressing or stifling our kids' words; we are talking about showing them how to direct their words in ways that are good for our kid and for those around them. We want them to show goodness through their speech, rather than jealousy or selfishness or anger.

Daily Response

1. How has your tongue-control been lately? Have you controlled your words or not?

2. How have your words been toward your children? Have you shown control or have your words been wild?

3. How can you teach your kid(s) to control their words? Is there any particular area where they've had a hard time in controlling what they say to others?

Gathering ending Week 6
Notes

SPECIAL GATHERING

Family Serve Experience

After about six weeks of going through *Jesus Embraced Parenting*, it is time for the Family Serve Experience. This is a time when the group (including kids) will go out and serve the community. You will have a chance to show the love of Christ through your service and model to your kids what it means to be the hands and feet of Jesus.

Where and When? This should be done at a separate time from the group's usual meeting. A Serve Experience usually takes 2-4 hours, depending on the activity chosen. It should be done sometime during either Week 6 or 7.

What Kind of Service? This is up to the group. Be creative. Take a risk, yet remember the ages of the kids that will be involved. You want to offer practical help that will bless others and allow you to interact with them.

Possible places to serve include: community food pantries, convalescent homes, soup kitchens, pregnancy counseling centers, group homes for the disabled or elderly, fire or police stations, helping at a community event, or other similar activities.

Important Reminders: Please keep the following in mind for your Serve Experience:
- This is meant to be *done as a group*, so do your best to pick a day/time when all can participate, including the kids.
- This is meant as an *outreach to others*, especially those who don't yet know Jesus. Serve the larger community, not just your own church family.
- This is meant to be *relational*, so talk to those you are serving. Ask questions and listen to their life stories. When possible, pray with them too.
- This is meant to be *kid-friendly*, so keep in mind your group's children as you plan. Provide them responsibilities that are appropriate for their ages. Kids usually love to help, especially in practical ways, so make sure they have "jobs" too.
- This is *real life* and not a ride at an amusement park. It isn't a controlled environment, so it might get messy. Unexpected things often happen while serving others, so be flexible to changes as needed. Just remember that you are there to

serve, so do your best at whatever you are asked to do that day.

Debrief: after the Serve Experience, your group should gather to *review and pray* about what you've just experienced. How did the experience challenge you? What did your children think about the experience?

Final Note: This activity is meant to encourage all of us parents to model to our children what it means to serve others. Hopefully, it will spur all of us to do such activities regularly as a family- helping those around us and showing the love of Jesus to them.

The Fruit of Faithfulness

But the fruit of the Spirit is love, joy, peace, forbearance, kindness, goodness, **faithfulness**, gentleness and self-control. Against such things there is no law. (Galatians 5:22-23 NIV *emphasis added*)

What is Faithfulness?

Broken Word

Amy: I loved my dad, but as a kid I learned that I couldn't depend on him to keep his word. He promised things and then failed to do them many times. Maybe it was his ADHD. Maybe it was forgetfulness. But as a kid you don't understand that there can be reasons for an adult to break their word. I learned to not believe his promises and to be self-reliant, because my dad wasn't being faithful. He didn't do it out of malice, but the result was the same: a distrust of his promises.

Earning Another's Faith

When faithfulness is mentioned as part of the fruit of the Spirit, the Bible isn't really focusing on a person's belief in God. By faithfulness, it means being a person of your word, being someone who is trustworthy. A person of faithfulness is someone to whom we can say "I have faith in you" and mean it.

As parents, we all want to be faithful toward our kids. We want them to trust that we will do everything we promise. We want them to look up to us as a parent, certain that we will keep our word, whether that's a promise of an ice cream or a trip to an amusement park. We want them to know we are dependable, and it hurts us almost as it does them whenever we fail to keep our word.

We also want our children to be known for being faithful themselves. We want to trust our kids and we want all those around them to do so too, but how do we model that to them?

In addition, how important is our trustworthiness to God?

Being Faithful with What We Have

Jesus told the story of three servants who were given money to invest for their master. Only trusted servants, who had proven themselves over many years, would have gotten such a responsibility. These three guys get a chance to show their master that his trust isn't misplaced, but one of them fails. One servant messes up and then tries to blame his master for his own failure:

"Again, it will be like a man going on a journey, who called his servants and entrusted his wealth to them. To one he gave five bags of gold, to another two bags, and to another one bag, each according to his ability. Then he went on his journey. The man who had received five bags of gold went at once and put his money to work and gained five bags more. So also, the one with two bags of gold gained two more. But the man who had received one bag went off, dug a hole in the ground and hid his master's money.

"After a long time the master of those servants returned and settled accounts with them. The man who had received five bags of gold brought the other five. 'Master,' he said, 'you entrusted me with five bags of gold. See, I have gained five more.'

"His master replied, 'Well done, good and faithful servant! You have been faithful with a few things; I will put you in charge of many things. Come and share your master's happiness!'

"The man with two bags of gold also came. 'Master,' he said, 'you entrusted me with two bags of gold; see, I have gained two more.'

"His master replied, 'Well done, good and faithful servant! You have been faithful with a few things; I will put you in charge of many things. Come and share your master's happiness!'

"Then the man who had received one bag of gold came. 'Master,' he said, 'I knew that you are a hard man, harvesting where you have not sown and gathering where you have not scattered seed. So I was afraid and went out and hid your gold in the ground. See, here is what belongs to you.'

"His master replied, 'You wicked, lazy servant! So you knew that I harvest where I have not sown and gather where I have not scattered seed? Well then, you should have put my money on deposit with the bankers, so that when I returned I would have received it back with interest.

" 'So take the bag of gold from him and give it to the one who has ten bags. For whoever has will be given more, and they will have an abundance. Whoever does not have, even what they have will be taken from them. And throw that worthless servant outside, into the darkness, where there will be weeping and gnashing of teeth.' (Matthew 25:14-30 NIV)

The third servant was unfaithful and then he slanders his master, claiming that he's a mean and unfair man. As readers, we need to be careful not to fall for this guy's lies, because he's trying to justify his failure by making his "boss" look like the bad guy. As the master said, even if the servant's lies had been truth, he could have at least put the gold into the bank to earn some interest instead of just burying the bag for safekeeping. The servant broke trust, proving himself unreliable.

The other two servants showed themselves faithful. They have varying levels of success but both are praised and given greater responsibilities in the household. They were faithful to their duties.

Meanwhile, that last servant couldn't be trusted anymore. Not only does the master revoke the servant's oversight of any money, he throws him out of the household and into the dark street where he will now face suffering. When we break trust, there are consequences.

What are We Doing with God's Riches?

The obvious question that we should ask after reading this parable is: have we been faithful in what God has entrusted to us? Have we been trustworthy servants or ones who just buried God's riches and then pretended it was God's fault that we did so.

What are the riches God has entrusted to us? Salvation is the first thing that comes to mind, but then comes all the rest that is our life in him: his blessings, his love, his spiritual gifts, his direction, his security, his resources, his comfort in hard times, his wisdom, and so on. Do we bury all of this, never doing anything with any of it? Or, do we invest the riches of God so that it grows greater in this world? Have we been a faithful follower of Jesus?

We need to remember that our master is going to return and he will ask what we did with all that he entrusted to us. Even while writing this, I (Eric) have to repent before our Lord because I haven't always been faithful with all that's he's given me. Has the love that he's given me grown or dwindled? Have I shared his abundant salvation with others or was I content to file that salvation in a security box like an insurance policy?

Have we invested all of it in our children? Have we taught our kids the importance of being faithful with what God has entrusted to them?

God expects an increase because he knows we are capable of doing so. Let's not disappoint him.

Daily Response

1. What are some of the riches that God has entrusted to you? How have you been faithful with those riches?

2. Sometimes, our kids need help in seeing how God has blessed them. What are some of the riches that you see in your kids' life? Try to list at least 5 for each child.

3. How can you encourage your kids to be more faithful toward others? How can you help them to be more trustworthy?

Keeping Our Word

Breaking My Word

Eric: I blew it. I had promised my wife a new barbecue for Spring, intending to replace a twenty-something built-in unit that had finally given up its last flame, but then I realized how much that would cost. Those built-in barbecues are expensive! I tried to find a cheaper unit or a way to convert a regular barbecue so that it would fit into the stone island on our patio, but those efforts only brought frustration. Weeks went by and we were still without a way to cook outdoors. Then our finances got too tight and other things came up, including a pandemic, and… well, I can give you a long list of excuses. The truth of it is that I broke my word. We didn't get a new barbecue. We went almost three years without any outdoor cooking.

I failed to keep my word to Amy. She was gracious enough to forgive me, but I never should have made a promise nor should I have failed to fulfill it.

Swearing to Prove our Word

"I swear to God…" is a common saying. We use it when we are trying to be emphatic about something. We want others to know that we are serious, so we add a swear to our statement.

- We might be threatening: "I swear to God- I'm going to get you."
- We might be claiming innocence: "I swear to God that I didn't do it."
- We might be trying to prove our honesty: "We just saw a movie star shopping at the discount store. I swear to God, we did."

In our desire to prove that we really mean what we're saying, we add that *swear*. Maybe we are doing this in business, trying to convince our boss that we will do a great job. Maybe we are swearing to our spouse or friends, trying to show our sincerity. Maybe we are doing this with our kids, hoping to convince them that we mean it this time. Often, we add in a "swear to God" because in the past, we haven't been faithful in our statements and promises.

Others have experienced our failures. We broke our word to them, so now we resort to more extravagant promises and vows, trying to show that we really mean it this time.

Even our kids can be swayed into swearing, from a seemingly-innocent pinky-promise swear as they interlock little fingers with their best buddy, to a more worrisome blood oath where kids cut their palms and then shake their blood-smeared hands.

However, Jesus orders us not to do any of this. Instead, he expects us to keep our answers simple and straightforward.

Keeping it Simple

In business, it is said that you should under-promise and over-deliver as a way to impress your customers. As Christians, we are encouraged to do neither. Instead, we are told to keep it to a simple answer, without any extravagant promises or any swearing that you'll do as you say. Just give them a straight answer. The Apostle James tells it this way:

> Above all, my brothers and sisters, do not swear—not by heaven or by earth or by anything else. All you need to say is a simple "Yes" or "No." Otherwise you will be condemned. (James 5:12 NIV)

James is building on what Jesus said, which is the following:

> "Again, you have heard that it was said to the people long ago, 'Do not break your oath, but fulfill to the Lord the vows you have made.' But I tell you, do not swear an oath at all: either by heaven, for it is God's throne; or by the earth, for it is his footstool; or by Jerusalem, for it is the city of the Great King. And do not swear by your head, for you cannot make even one hair white or black. All you need to say is simply 'Yes' or 'No'; anything beyond this comes from the evil one.
> (Matthew 5:33-37 NIV)

How often have we felt pressured to offer someone more than a simple yes or no? We want to be believed. We want to impress the other person with our passion and zeal. Then we give in, and do what Jesus tells us not to do. We swear an oath to show our commitment, and in doing so we sin.

Promises Kept

This year, I (Eric) finally fulfilled that years-old promise of an outdoor grill. We went out as a family and bought a new barbecue. Our boys were very excited about it and couldn't wait to help cook with fire! (Now if they would only be so eager to help with regular dinners…) I finally made good and kept my word.

I think all of us want to be people of our word. We especially want our kids to know that they can count on us, that we won't let them down. We mean well, as I did when I promised to buy a replacement grill years ago, but then we fail to come through. That is another reason why it is best to keep our answers to a simple yes or no, leaving off the elaborate promises and the swearing of oaths. That is especially true when we are dealing with our kids.

Jesus wants us to be parents of integrity, and that includes having integrity in our words.

Daily Response

1. Have you ever gone beyond a simple "yes" or "no"? How so?

2. How can you improve at keeping your word with others (especially your kids)?

3. How can you help your kids to be better at keeping their word, rather than making elaborate promises that they can't fulfill?

WEEK 7	DAY 3

Work Responsibility

Hire and Fire

Eric: I've hired and fired hundreds of people. I don't say that to brag or to apologize; I'm just stating a fact. I've worked in industries where there's high employee turnover, so I've had to hire and fire people for many years and in many different states of the USA. All those people weren't my own staff- they worked for the companies and clients that I worked for. (Even as I write this, I'm working with a client- a construction company- to hire new staff, running ads, reviewing dozens of applications, and helping conduct interviews.)

Over the years, I've had many new hires who turned out to be fantastic employees, while others were real stinkers. You can't always tell what you'll get based on resumes, skill tests, references, and interviews. It takes time, seeing the person actually work, to determine if someone is a great worker or not. They have to show that they are faithful to their job responsibilities.

I have fired people for excessive absenteeism, working another job while on-the-clock, poor performance, theft, falsification of records, sexual harassment, violating safety protocols, and many other reasons. Sadly, there are people out there who have no sense of responsibility when it comes to their jobs.

Our boys aren't old enough to go out for job interviews yet, but we still want them to learn what it means to be a trustworthy worker. Each one has his own "job list" on the fridge, which shows the daily and weekly tasks that are expected of them. Their weekly "salaries" are determined by how faithful they are in completing those assignments. Amy and I want our sons to learn to be faithful in their work.

Diligent

Amy and I want our children to learn how to be diligent. That's an old-fashioned word, but it fits so well. Diligent, as in hard-working, careful to complete, thorough in a task. What a great attribute for our kids to learn. A diligent worker is the one who will impress the boss and the customer. A diligent worker will gain a good reputation with co-workers and clients both. Who wouldn't want their kids to attain that?

However, teaching our kids to be responsible workers isn't always easy. When they're little, it takes so much patience whenever we "let them do it themselves", be that making a bed, pulling weeds, or vacuuming the living room. Young children are often eager to help, but so slow and in need of so much coaching on how to get it right.

When they're older we often face more reluctance. It is often seems easier to do it ourselves rather than nag them to do their assigned work, but when we let them get away with slacking off, we are failing at our own job. As parents, our job isn't to make their bed or wash their clothes; our job is to teach them how to make a bed and wash clothes.

Earning Respect

Timothy was a young guy just starting in his profession. As often happens, he encountered resistance, especially because he was in a position of authority at such a young age. Paul considered him the son he never had, so the older man did his best to give him advice, especially since he was following in Paul's footsteps to be a minister.

> Don't let anyone look down on you because you are young, but set an example for the believers in speech, in conduct, in love, in faith and in purity. Until I come, devote yourself to the public reading of Scripture, to preaching and to teaching. Do not neglect your gift, which was given you through prophecy when the body of elders laid their hands on you.
>
> Be diligent in these matters; give yourself wholly to them, so that everyone may see your progress. Watch your life and doctrine closely. Persevere in them, because if you do, you will save both yourself and your hearers. (1 Timothy 4:12-16 NIV)

Paul's advice is sound, no matter what kind of job our kids have started.
1. Expect respect by setting an example to others (v. 12)
2. Devote yourself to what's important for the job (v. 13)
3. Don't neglect how God has gifted you (v. 14)
4. Be diligent and fully committed to what you are doing (v. 15)
5. Watch to make sure your life and beliefs stay true and in balance (v. 16)
6. Persevere, for your own sake and for others (v. 16)

Our kids' first job might not be anything as important as Timothy's, but if they learn to apply the 6 points above it will take them far in life. They will learn to work diligently while still remaining true to who they are and how God has gifted them.

Faithful in your Work

Amy and I are not advocating for becoming workaholics; that's an unhealthy lifestyle that will hurt you and your family. However, the fruit of faithfulness is all about being a person of your *word*, of taking responsibility and seeing things through to completion.

When we are faithful in our work, we set a good example for our kids. When they see a healthy, balance-yet-focused approach to work, they will have a better idea of what to expect from their future career.

Daily Response

1. What does "being diligent" look like in your life?

2. Amy often prays for children's "jobs", by which she means their educational career, whether they are in 1st grade, middle school, or even college. How can you encourage your kids to work diligently at their job of learning?

3. In addition to school, your kids probably have chores at home that they are expected to complete regularly. If your kids are older, then they may also have some volunteer responsibilities, clubs, sports, or even a part-time paying job. List out your kids' current "jobs" and then consider how you can encourage them to be diligent in each job.

Financial Responsibility

Pay Up

Eric: "I want $20 to clean my room," announced one of my kids. He only needed a bit more money so that he could buy something he'd been wanting for many weeks, so he thought he could get it all with one large project. To his mind it was the perfect solution, his parents would be happy with a cleaner house and he would be happy with a wad of cash. He wanted us to provide a quick fix to his financial needs.

The only problem was that neither Mom nor Dad was about to pay those kind of wages, especially when he wanted it for cleaning up a mess he made in the first place.

He was disappointed when we wouldn't agree to his deal, and he was even more bummed when we explained what he would have to do to earn that kind of money. Our son wanted to get that money and he wanted us to make it happen in the quickest, least laborious way.

To be honest, Amy and I have been guilty of doing the same thing with God. Looking back over our life together, there have been numerous times we've messed up financially and then looked to God for a solution. We let credit card debt grow to thousands of dollars. We failed to stick to a family budget. We didn't keep our emergency fund full, then something unexpected wiped out all that was left and more. We would lose sleep over our finances, calling out to God for wisdom and relief. Our prayers were sincere, but it was also true that we really wanted God to provide a quick fix. A big wad of cash would be great, God.

Money Crunch

Almost all of us have gotten ourselves into a financial bind at some time in our life. Maybe we took on too much debt. Maybe we bought something far too expensive and then struggled with big payments. Maybe we let others take advantage of us and now we are stuck with their debt. Money problems can really strain a marriage, a friendship, and a parent-child relationship.

When we don't have our own finances in order, it can be harder to teach our kids to do better. Feeling guilty or inadequate, we fail to take the time to show them how to save money, to balance a checking account, pay off a credit card each month, or how to watch out for excessive interest rates.

Work Hard and Avoid Financial Traps

Sometimes we get into financial trouble because of others. We try to help them out and we cause our own finances to suffer. We aren't talking about charity or giving to the poor; we are talking about letting others take advantage of us. Sometimes, the person who is taking advantage of us is our own kid, which isn't good for them or us. We need to have financial responsibility. It's a lesson we need to learn as parents and also teach to our children.

Our personal word counts, so we shouldn't be quick to endorse someone or co-sign their loan, or we might live to regret it. The Proverbs dad warns his son that if he ever made that mistake he needs to immediately do everything he can to get out of it, even if that means getting a second job or working lots of overtime. He'll need to get himself out of that financial trap as fast as he can before it ruins him.

> My son, if you have put up security for your neighbor, if you have shaken hands in pledge for a stranger, you have been trapped by what you said, ensnared by the words of your mouth. So do this, my son, to free yourself, since you have fallen into your neighbor's hands: Go—to the point of exhaustion— and give your neighbor no rest! Allow no sleep to your eyes, no slumber to your eyelids. Free yourself, like a gazelle from the hand of the hunter, like a bird from the snare of the fowler.
>
> Go to the ant, you sluggard; consider its ways and be wise! It has no commander, no overseer or ruler, yet it stores its provisions in summer and gathers its food at harvest.
>
> How long will you lie there, you sluggard? When will you get up from your sleep? A little sleep, a little slumber, a little folding of the hands to rest— and poverty will come on you like a thief and scarcity like an armed man. (Proverbs 6:1-13 NIV)

The Proverbs dad pushes hard on his son to get out of bad debts. He doesn't want his son to be a sluggard who lets those debts overtake him in his sleep. He doesn't want his son to end up poor, so his words get harsh to get his point across. That trapped gazelle or bird will be desperate to break away from the hunter; the animal will do anything to be free again. His son needs to be just as focused on getting out of financial snares.

He also wants his son to plan ahead like an ant, even if there isn't anyone telling him to do so, and plan for the tougher times ahead.

Be Content with What you Have

Our society encourages discontent. "Don't be happy with your life as it is now, when you could have _____." We need to buy, watch, experience, eat, drink, wear, visit, and drive whatever the marketers are pushing. They grow rich on the sins that they encourage in us; they make their money and we get to battle with sins like lust, greed, jealousy, and envy.

However, the Bible urges another attitude. Paul, writing to Timothy (whom he considered to be like a son to him), said the following:

> But godliness with contentment is great gain. For we brought nothing into the world, and we can take nothing out of it. But if we have food and clothing, we will be content with that. Those who want to get rich fall into temptation and a trap and into many foolish and harmful desires that plunge people into ruin and destruction. For the love of money is a root of all kinds of evil. Some people, eager for money, have wandered from the faith and pierced themselves with many griefs.
> (1 Timothy 6:6-10 NIV)

Many have misquoted the above verse and claimed that "money is the root of all evil", as if it's a sin to be rich, but that isn't what Paul is warning Timothy about. He's warning about those who let greed take over.

Learning about Money

Money is a huge thing for most of us. No matter how much we make or have, we usually think it's not enough, which is why it can be such a huge temptation that will mess up our faith. Just like Paul told his spiritual son, Timothy, lusting for money is a cause for all kinds of evil.

Teaching our children about Jesus is our most important task, but teaching them financial responsibility is probably in the top 5 lessons we can give them. If they have a healthy attitude toward money, our kids will be spared from so many disappointments and temptations.

Daily Response

1. What have you done to teach your children about money and how to handle it wisely?

2. How can you teach your kids the importance of not being greedy but instead giving to others, like to ministry, to the poor, and to those in crisis?

3. How can you teach your children the importance of not falling in love with money?

Breaking Faith:
Lies and Deceit

Friends Who Lie

Amy: There was this girl that I met at church summer camp who became what I thought was a good friend... until I realized that she wasn't. Although we didn't go to the same schools, we attended the same church through our teen years. She was friendly and fun to hang out with, but slowly I realized that her many stories weren't true. She would brag about non-existent relationships. Starved for male attention, she would pretend certain guys were flirting with her even though in reality the guys had no interest in her whatsoever. My "friend" was living a life of deception and it just got worse as the years went by. She believed that those lies were true, that the pretend stories were really the life she was living.

Lying destroyed our relationship, because I realized I couldn't have any faith in anything she said. I finally ended the friendship because it had become toxic.

Chronic Liars

We have all probably had a co-worker, neighbor, friend, or loved one who lied regularly. We can't trust any kind of relationship that might be there, because at least half of that relationship is built on the unstable sand of deception. Do they really mean what they said? Are they gossiping behind our back too? Are they just telling us what we want to hear, instead of the truth? We can't trust them because they are not people of their word; they aren't faithful to the truth.

Honestly, without some serious intervention and yielding to the Spirit's conviction, such people won't change.

Beware of the Deceivers in Church

Paul talks about confronting the ones who aren't faithful, especially among us Christians.

> I urge you, brothers and sisters, to watch out for those who cause divisions and put obstacles in your way that are contrary to the teaching you have learned. Keep away from them. For such people are not serving our Lord Christ, but their own appetites. By smooth talk and flattery they deceive the minds of naive people. Everyone has heard about your obedience, so I rejoice because of you; but I want you to be wise about what is good, and innocent about what is evil.
>
> The God of peace will soon crush Satan under your feet.
>
> The grace of our Lord Jesus be with you. (Romans 16:17-20 NIV)

Paul is warning that there will be people in the church that will cause problems, teach lies, and create obstacles to keep us or our children from knowing and living out the Christian life. They are doing it to feed "their own appetites", but they can seem so convincing, so genuine at times with their dynamic personality and their flattery. This person might be a newcomer or someone you've seen at church for years, it could be a visiting speaker or even a church leader gone rogue. Whoever they are, they're trying to manipulate us or our children to their own purpose, and it's not always so obvious. They are breaking faith with us and our Lord by pursuing their own needs and appetites instead of pursuing Jesus and the good of his Kingdom. Paul tells us to keep away from them.

Avoid the Deceivers

We should avoid the kind of people that Paul talks about, and we should get our kids away from them too. We need to learn how to choose our friends and companions wisely and we need to teach our kids to do the same.

We need to be aware who is around our kids. Who is influencing them at church, at school, on a sports team, in a club, in online communities, or in the neighborhood? We need to show them how to funnel all these people through a filter of whether these other kids or adults are helpful or are they toxic?

Daily Response

1. Have you ever been around a toxic person? How did you realize that they weren't healthy to be around?

2. How can you learn about the kids and adults influencing your child?

3. How can you teach your kid to funnel and filter their peers and keep only the ones who are healthy for them?

Gathering ending Week 7
Notes

The Fruit of Gentleness

But the fruit of the Spirit is love, joy, peace, forbearance, kindness, goodness, faithfulness, **gentleness** and self-control. Against such things there is no law. (Galatians 5:22-23 NIV *emphasis added*)

What is Gentleness?

Scary or Gentle?

Eric: "Roar!" I yelled, hands lifted like two huge claws in front of me. The kids screamed and ran, but they also laughed. They fled into one of the bedrooms and slammed the door shut, having escaped the monster. They were safe in their make-believe fortress.

I stomped and huffed in the hallway. I scratched and banged on the door. I even tried to plea for them to come out, promising to be a better monster and not eat them. They were not fooled.

I retreated to hide behind another door and waited. Soon, they were peeking out to see what had happened to the brutish beast. Egging each other on, they crept out, looking everywhere but not finding me.

Waiting for them to get near, I suddenly jumped out with a loud roar.

They screamed and ran for the bedroom fortress, enjoying the scare.

Make-believe monsters are fun, but real ones aren't. My kids will laugh when I'm a pretend beast roaring loudly, but they certainly don't enjoy it whenever I'm loud because of frustration or anger, even if such occasions are rare and even if they aren't the focus of my frustration. In real life, they prefer an even-tempered, measured response. They prefer calm over upset.

In real life, they want gentleness in their dad.

Gentleness Misunderstood

Gentleness is a fruit of the Spirit that is rather underrated. Our society often makes fun of gentleness, seeing it as a sign of weakness. Sadly, even some Christians have mocked gentleness, trying to remake Jesus as a tough guy more likely to ride a window-rattling motorcycle to a bar fight than to ride a humble donkey to his death on a cross. They want Jesus to be an angry rebel rather than a loving servant.

To some of us, the idea of Jesus being gentle is embarrassing, which means that maybe we don't really understand what it means to be gentle.

Measured Response

Seeking to trap Jesus, religious leaders brought a woman to him, claiming they had caught her in the act of adultery (notice that they didn't bring the man). There was no gentleness in their treatment of her, nor in their attempted treatment of Jesus. The old Jewish law said adulterers were to be killed for their sin, so they wanted to either force Jesus to order her death or have him defy the law. They wanted this to be a lose-lose situation.

> At dawn he appeared again in the temple courts, where all the people gathered around him, and he sat down to teach them. The teachers of the law and the Pharisees brought in a woman caught in adultery. They made her stand before the group and said to Jesus, "Teacher, this woman was caught in the act of adultery. In the Law Moses commanded us to stone such women. Now what do you say?" They were using this question as a trap, in order to have a basis for accusing him.
>
> But Jesus bent down and started to write on the ground with his finger. When they kept on questioning him, he straightened up and said to them, "Let any one of you who is without sin be the first to throw a stone at her." Again he stooped down and wrote on the ground.
>
> At this, those who heard began to go away one at a time, the older ones first, until only Jesus was left, with the woman still standing there. Jesus straightened up and asked her, "Woman, where are they? Has no one condemned you?"
>
> "No one, sir," she said.
>
> "Then neither do I condemn you," Jesus declared. "Go now and leave your life of sin."
>
> (John 8:2-11 NIV)

Jesus was gentle with the men. He responded calmly to their angry accusations and scheming. In his gentleness, he forced them to recognize that they too deserved to be stoned to death, for they were just as guilty as she was. Jesus could have named names. He could have revealed their sins in front of that crowd, but instead he calmly told them to go ahead and kill her if they were sinless themselves. Convicted of their own sin, one after the other slipped away, forgetting about their schemes.

His gentleness brought conviction.

Jesus was also gentle with the woman. He refused to condemn her, but instead told her to stop leading a life of sin. Interestingly, she could have fled as soon as her accusers slipped away, but Jesus' gentleness seemed to keep her there. His gentleness caused her to linger, even though there wasn't anybody there to restrain her. When Jesus stood up and looked at her, she must have known that he knew she was guilty, but she still stayed to hear what he had to say.

Jesus didn't approve of her sins, but neither did he condemn her to death for them. Instead, he gently forgave her and told her to repent- to change her ways.

His gentleness brought forgiveness and repentance.

Facing Attacks of Others

As believers, we are called to be gentle even when we are being attacked for doing good. You have to be tough to be able to show gentleness and respect toward those who are mocking your faith, but that is what we are expected to do:

> Who is going to harm you if you are eager to do good? But even if you should suffer for what is right, you are blessed. "Do not fear their threats; do not be frightened." But in your hearts revere Christ as Lord. Always be prepared to give an answer to everyone who asks you to give the reason for the hope that you have. But do this with gentleness and respect, keeping a clear conscience, so that those who speak maliciously against your good behavior in Christ may be ashamed of their slander. (1 Peter 3:13-16 NIV)

Being gentle in the face of verbal attacks will make us stand out. The world around us would never do that, but we are called to be like Jesus. As parents, we are also called to teach our children to act like Jesus too.

Gently Influential

If we want to have true influence on those around us (especially our kids), we need to learn to be gentle. We don't earn the respect of others by roaring like a monster or scheming to trap others in their words or sins. We earn respect with gentle truth, with a measured response and loving call to repentance.

Daily Response

1. Think about a situation in your life where gentleness was needed. Did you show gentleness or not?

2. Have you ever been attacked or mocked for showing gentleness?

3. How can you model gentleness to your kids?

Forgiving Others

I'm Sorry

Eric: In our household we try to deal with sin and grievances quickly. Amy often talks about keeping "short accounts", about not letting that sin fester between two people. She sets the example for the rest of us, always being quick to apologize for any offense. I'm not as fast at admitting my wrongs or at dealing with the consequences, but I'm much better at it after seeing Amy model it consistently year after year.

Our kids also understand the principle of apologizing when they do something wrong, however they don't always mean what they say. I don't know how many times I've heard "I'm sorry" in a tone that implies the speaker really isn't sorry for anything. Sometimes the words are sung in a chipper voice that sounds not-the-least-regretting. Sometimes "I'm sorry" is spat out like the words are poisoning the speaker's tongue. The offender claims to be apologizing, but there's no obvious signs of remorse or admitting to doing wrong. It feels like they have no intention of changing their ways. They are acting like "I'm sorry" is a magical phrase that makes everything okay again.

On the other side, I've also heard many grumbled "I forgive you" responses that sure didn't sound like they had forgiven anything. Sometimes it is understandable, since the offending kid obviously isn't really sorry for what they did, but sometimes there is genuine repentance and yet the other kid doesn't want to let it go. There is still a desire for punishment, for making the offender pay for his crimes.

How do I get my kids to mean what they say? How can I encourage them to really forgive?

When Someone Wrongs Us

Forgiving someone when they've wronged us is hard to do. All of us have experienced being hurt by someone else, and usually we want to respond by hurting them in return. We want revenge or justice or judgment. We want that other person to face a comparable suffering for what they did.

But we are supposed to leave vengeance for God. He's the only one who fully understands everything. He's the only one who can provide perfect justice. Admittedly, it isn't always easy to trust him to take care of it for us, but that lack of trust is mainly because we haven't spent enough time to know our Lord's heart. He really cares about us and wants what is best for us. He knows that learning to forgive others is for our emotional health. He wants us to let go of the resentment, the fear, and the bitterness that build up from being unforgiving.

Right Way to Forgive

What is the right way to forgive others? First, we need to realize that forgiving others isn't optional. Matthew, right after recording the Lord's Prayer, shares this from Jesus:

> For if you forgive other people when they sin against you, your heavenly Father will also forgive you. But if you do not forgive others their sins, your Father will not forgive your sins. (Matthew 6:14-15 NIV)

That's hard to hear sometimes, but that's what Jesus said. We must forgive and then God forgives us. When we can't release others of their wrongs, how can God free of us of ours? We free ourselves by letting go of others.

Think of it as the shackles of a prisoner. Sin causes those chains of bondage between two people. It binds up both the sinner and the one sinned against. When we forgive, we unlock the chain on our end. (The sinner still needs to deal with their end- but that's not our direct concern.) How can God really set us free if we are refusing to unlock that binding chain by forgiving the other person?

Sin Among the Family of God

The Apostle Paul realizes that there will still be sin between fellow Christians and that we need to learn how to deal with that sin correctly.

> Therefore, as God's chosen people, holy and dearly loved, clothe yourselves with compassion, kindness, humility, gentleness and patience. Bear with each other and forgive one another if any of you has a grievance against someone. Forgive as the Lord forgave you. And over all these virtues put on love, which binds them all together in perfect unity. (Colossians 3:12-14 NIV)

We are to forgive our fellow Christians like Jesus forgave us, which was completely and sacrificially. He didn't ignore our sins nor did he make excuses for our sins. Instead, Jesus knew the seriousness of our wrongdoing and yet still forgave. When we are having a hard time showing forgiveness, we often need to be reminded of how Jesus forgave us for everything.

Our children are to forgive like Jesus too, but that's something they need to learn how to do. It doesn't mean winking at wrongs or ignoring incidents; Jesus confronted sin as necessary. Hopefully, our kids will learn from us.

We and our kids need to see the awfulness of the sin but still should be ready to forgive when the sinner repents. We should bear with others, letting go of any grievances, and instead being compassionate, kind, humble, gentle and patient with that other person. We are to love. We need to remember that we aren't that different from them:

> Brothers and sisters, if someone is caught in a sin, you who live by the Spirit should restore that person gently. But watch yourselves, or you also may be tempted. Carry each other's burdens, and in this way you will fulfill the law of Christ. (Galatians 6:1-2 NIV)

Paul's advice is practical for any group of Christians, whether it be at your local church or in your own household. We forgive as we help the sinner deal with the sin they've done.

1. **Don't ignore:** When we are aware of someone sinning (whether against us or against another), we shouldn't pretend to not notice it. As parents, ignoring the wrong doesn't help our kids, because they miss the chance to repent and get it right. Healthy confrontation of sin is a good thing for us to model to our kids too, because they might be prone to want to ignore sin too.

2. **Our aim is to restore**, not to condemn. We should want to see that our kids get right with God and others, not to make them suffer. Often people need to face the consequences of their wrongs to really learn from them, but "facing the consequences" shouldn't be our goal for the sinner we're dealing with. We want our kids to be restored in their relationship with God, with us, with their siblings, with their friends, and with anyone else where sin has messed things up.

3. **Use gentleness:** We aren't here to shame them or overwhelm them with our greater presence. We are to use gentleness to win them over to repentance. In the same way, our kids need to learn how to help others toward repentance- not by bullying younger siblings or embarrassing classmates. By using gentleness, we are more likely to be heard by others.

4. **Be careful of our own temptations:** We are to deal with the messes of our kids with gentleness, being careful that we aren't tempted to sin ourselves. Maybe we won't be tempted to do the exact same sin, but their sin might tempt us to the sin of rage or gossip or mocking. Another's sin can temp us into our own sin, be it the same thing or not.

The same can happen with our kids when they are dealing with someone else's sin. They need to be aware that it can be dangerous being around another's sin.

Carefully Let It Go

Sin is a serious thing, even in our kids' lives. Sin will affect them- their own sins and the sins of others. It can't be avoided so it is best to deal with it as quickly as possible. We need to teach them how to keep these things from festering, because sin not dealt with will twist in us.

One last thing comes to mind when dealing with forgiving sin: not everyone wants to be forgiven because some don't want to admit they did anything wrong. We need to realize this and so do our kids: some people will never ask for forgiveness from God or from people, but that doesn't mean we shouldn't offer it to them nonetheless.

Jesus is so extravagant in the forgiveness he provides at the cross- he loved the whole world and offered that forgiveness to everyone, even though he knew many would refuse his gift. We, too, are called to be extravagant in forgiving others, but we also need to realize not everyone will take the forgiveness we offer.

Daily Response

1. Did you offer forgiveness to anyone this week? What did that look like?

2. How would you use Paul's 4 steps to restore your child after they sin?

3. How can you tea your kid to forgive others?

Loving in Discipline

Tantrum to Tears

Amy: My first memory of my dad was when I was a preschooler and I had a friend over to the house. My little friend showed me how to throw a temper tantrum, and it was fun and we were loud. Just imagine: two girls screaming at the top of their lungs over and over again.

My dad looked in and told us to stop.

We didn't.

He warned us a second time.

We couldn't resist. Screaming was just too much fun.

Furious, my dad stormed into the room and grabbed me, dragging me to the bathroom. He pulled down my pants and started whacking me on my butt with a toilet bowl brush- the nearest switch he could find. My mother had to intervene to stop the beating.

I learned my lesson and never threw a temper tantrum again. Sadly, I also learned to fear my dad whenever he became mad.

The Struggle is Real

We all struggle with anger. Our kids seem to know how to push our buttons, especially whenever we are tired or frazzled. Sometimes it feels like they are just begging for punishment. We take what they are doing as personal; we turn it into an offense against us.

We want our kids to behave. We want them to lovingly respect us by doing what we say without delay and with a joyful attitude. It can really offend us when they don't.

For some of us, that anger happens far too often, and we're reacting inappropriately to our kids' misbehavior. It's not healthy.

Care Enough to Correct

Discipline is far more than a spanking or a time-out. Discipline is training someone on how to "do" right. Discipline in the military or the gym includes the idea of striving to improve. The person disciplining (be it a drill sergeant or a personal coach) is modeling and teaching others how to do something right. A good discipliner isn't just chewing you out for your errors and shortcomings; they are explaining how to do it correctly. It's kind of like a mentor and student relationship- both participate for it to be truly effective. Hopefully, the disciplining is being done with the right attitude as well.

In the book of Hebrews, we learn that God's discipline of us is done out of his love for us.

> In your struggle against sin, you have not yet resisted to the point of shedding your blood. And have you completely forgotten this word of encouragement that addresses you as a father addresses his son? It says,
> "My son, do not make light of the Lord's discipline,
> and do not lose heart when he rebukes you,
> because the Lord disciplines the one he loves,
> and he chastens everyone he accepts as his son."
> Endure hardship as discipline; God is treating you as his children. For what children are not disciplined by their father? If you are not disciplined—and everyone undergoes discipline—then you are not legitimate, not true sons and daughters at all. Moreover, we have all had human fathers who disciplined us and we respected them for it. How much more should we submit to the Father of spirits and live! They disciplined us for a little while as they thought best; but God disciplines us for our good, in order that we may share in his holiness. No discipline seems pleasant at the time, but painful. Later on, however, it produces a harvest of righteousness and peace for those who have been trained by it (Hebrews 12:4-11 NIV)

React or Respond

Obviously, my story of being a preschooler practicing tantrums is an example of how not to discipline your child. My dad let his anger get the better of him, reacting swiftly when the screaming became too much for him. He started whacking me with nearest object he could find. This is a misapplication of the scripture, "spare the rod and spoil the child".

Getting angry is not necessarily a sin. However, when we just **react** to what our kids are doing, we are more prone to sin ourselves. When we do something quick, letting our emotions have control, we often make mistakes. What we need to do instead, is **respond** to their misbehavior. Pause to let our adrenaline or anger lower and really assess the situation. We may have to rush in to prevent a real catastrophe (anything to do with fire, electricity, rushing water, or a hissing cat comes to mind), but then we need to catch our breath and really think about what we are going to say or do next. We need to decide what is the best option to correct the behavior. We need to find an effective way to discipline- not to punish or get retribution, but to teach them what's wrong and what's right.

Each child responds differently. I (Amy) was a fairly compliant child, so my dad's over-the-top swatting still worked to teach me that tantrums (whether fake or real) would not be allowed in our home. If I were to try that with my own kids, it probably wouldn't work

The goal of discipline is not to overpower our kid and force our will upon them. (Scriptures tell us not to exasperate our child.) The goal is to discipline our child into becoming a successful person who will someday be an adult who knows that there are consequences to inappropriate behavior. If we love our kids, we will take the time to discipline them for their sake.

Daily Response

1. What are some things you can do to make sure that you are *responding* rather than just *reacting* to your kids' misbehavior? (Time out for them, waiting before deciding on a punishment, etc.)

2. How can you be loving in your disciplining?

3. Is corporal punishment (spanking, swatting, etc.) ever appropriate? Why or why not?

Sweet Unity

When two people don't function as one.

Amy: I grew up in a home where my parents argued constantly, especially over money. Both my mom and my dad would spend on all sorts of stuff for themselves but never talked it over with each other. There was no accountability and no communication. They rarely had any goals to save toward (they couldn't even save for their only child's wedding), so the money was spent haphazardly, with no real purpose other than to gratify immediate desires.

They spent behind each other's back and then yelled at the other person for doing the same thing. It caused a lot of chaos in my childhood home, just because my parents couldn't work as a team.

Missing Parental Unity

Being united as parents is so vital- united in our priorities, our spending, our kid-raising, and our time commitments. But so often that unity is lacking. We might not be yellers like my (Amy's) parents, but that teamwork attitude isn't there. The disunity might show up in a different way, but it still causes frustration and tension in the household. Our kids will still sense it.

What Jesus Wants for Us

Do you realize that Jesus prayed for you and it is recorded in the Bible? The Apostle John wrote it down. Jesus was praying about his quickly-approaching crucifixion, then he continued by praying for the disciples that had been following him all over Judea and Galilee, and finally he prayed for you (and the rest of us). This is what Jesus said:

> "My prayer is not for them alone. I pray also for those who will believe
> in me through their message, that all of them may be one, Father, just as
> you are in me and I am in you. May they also be in us so that the world

may believe that you have sent me. I have given them the glory that you gave me, that they may be one as we are one—I in them and you in me—so that they may be brought to complete unity. Then the world will know that you sent me and have loved them even as you have loved me." (John 17:20-23 NIV)

Jesus prayed that we would have unity in God. It's that important to him. He wants us to have unity with our fellow believers, and that especially includes our spouse.

Starting from the first book in the Bible, marriage is described as uniting two people to become one. "That is why a man leaves his father and mother and is united to his wife, and they become one flesh." (Genesis 2:24 NIV) Jesus expanded on that when he was being quizzed about divorce laws:

> "It was because your hearts were hard that Moses wrote you this law," Jesus replied. "But at the beginning of creation God 'made them male and female.' 'For this reason a man will leave his father and mother and be united to his wife, and the two will become one flesh.' So they are no longer two, but one flesh. Therefore what God has joined together, let no one separate."
> (Mark 10:5-9 NIV)

The more united parents are the more they are reflecting God to their kids, because God is a god of love and unity. When you are united with each other for the common good of the children, you are showing God to them.

Two is Best

Parenting works best as a team sport- with a husband and wife working in unity to raise their kids. Unfortunately, there are a lot of parents who don't have that best scenario to work with.

We understand that not everyone going through this study is married: some are single parents, some widowed, some separated, and some divorced. We also understand that not all of you are married to the other parent of your child and are maybe sharing custody. In addition, some of you are a step-parent, grandparent, or other relative or friend who is helping to raise a child. In spite of all that, it is important that we talk about how parents (married or not) ought to be united.

Please do your best to adapt to your life situation and find as much unity as possible between you and any other adult involved in raising your child. They are worth the effort.

Daily Response

1. How does unity help with parenting your children?

2. What is one area where you would like to have greater unity in raising your children?

3. What are some ways you can model and teach *unity* to your kids?

Encouraging our Kids

Forgotten

Amy: Birthdays are so important to all of us, especially when we are young kids. In elementary school, our boys were used to having the teacher acknowledge their birthday with a brief announcement. However, our one son has a late summer birthday, coming only days after the start of the school year, and one year his teacher forgot to acknowledge his special day.

He was crushed.

She forgot and said nothing about him on that day (although she acknowledged his birthday a week later along with some others), so he soured toward school from then on. Years later, he still remembers the experience of being forgotten.

Discouraged

How many of us have felt unnoticed or overlooked? It can drain our motivation. We can feel like we don't matter, or maybe we were even told we don't. Our courage to even try gets drained from us; we become discouraged.

As parents, in our frustration or impatience, we can sometimes make our own kids feel like they are an afterthought to our priorities. We don't listen. We don't acknowledge them. We're too occupied dealing with our own hurts to even notice theirs. We are too busy rushing through whatever needs to be done to take time for them. It shouldn't happen like that, but sometimes it does. So, what would be a more godly approach?

Building Up Others

The Bible provides an answer to our conundrum. When we remember that our kids are also our fellow believers, we can better apply Scriptures like the following:

> He died for us so that, whether we are awake or asleep, we may live together with him. Therefore encourage one another and build each other

up, just as in fact you are doing.

Now we ask you, brothers and sisters, to acknowledge those who work hard among you, who care for you in the Lord and who admonish you. Hold them in the highest regard in love because of their work. Live in peace with each other. And we urge you, brothers and sisters, warn those who are idle and disruptive, encourage the disheartened, help the weak, be patient with everyone. Make sure that nobody pays back wrong for wrong, but always strive to do what is good for each other and for everyone else. (1 Thessalonians 5: 10-15 NIV)

We are getting a good game plan on how to interact with our children:
1.   Encourage and build up (We need to to encourage our kids)
2.   Acknowledge those working hard in their spiritual calling (God has specially gifted them; we need to acknowledge that whenever we see it in action)
3.   Live in peace with each other
4.   Warn those who are idle (chores and homework still need to get done)
5.   Warn those who are disruptive (they need to learn how to get along in your family, in school, and in larger society)
6.   Don't take retribution or revenge (we should never do this and neither should they)
7.   Do what is good for each other

All of these things revolve around encouraging our kids to be who God created them to be- how He gifted them uniquely.

Catching them Doing Good

Sometimes parenthood can turn negative, where the only thing we seem to be doing is telling our kids "no". It might be for good reason (Get down from the roof! Don't eat that! The cat doesn't need a shave.), but our kids need more than a behavior cop. They need a mentor, a cheerleader, and a positive role model, and that's us too.

We need to notice when our kids have done something good and we ought to praise them for it. They hunger for that from us. When they are younger, they are more open about that desire for our praise- showing us their latest drawing or LEGO build or clothing choices. As they get older, they might not be so willing to ask for our praise, but they want it just as much. We need to be extravagant in celebrating what makes our kids' special, doing it as often and as creatively as we can, and doing it in ways they appreciate the most, whether that's in words, hugs, prizes, or lots of smiles and tears of happiness.

Daily Response

1. Can you think of any time where you were forgotten or overlooked by others? How did that make you feel?

2. Look back at the previous page and reread 1 Thessalonians 5 as well as the 7 points listed. What are the 2 or 3 things you would want to do better with your kids?

3. How do your kids most appreciate your praise and encouragement? Is it in words, actions, gifts, time with you, or in lots of hugs and kisses? What is the best way for you to show your encouragement to them?

Gathering ending Week 8
Notes

The Fruit of Self-Control

But the fruit of the Spirit is love, joy, peace, forbearance, kindness, goodness, faithfulness, gentleness and **self-control**. Against such things there is no law. (Galatians 5:22-23 NIV *emphasis added*)

What is Self-Control?

Losing Control

Eric: We have a loved one who suffers from trauma-induced epilepsy. If she misses her medication, she begins to have seizures. Have you ever seen someone having a seizure? The person loses control of their body, shaking violently. It is a frightening thing to watch. You feel helpless when the seizures start, because there's nothing you can do to stop an episode.

Amy and I have experienced a similar feeling when talking with friends who have an out-of-control teen or young adult. We listen and we share with the parents what we can, but we still feel helpless as all of us watch their child careen into a lot of pain and suffering. These teens and young adults are experiencing not lack of body-control (like our epileptic loved one), but are suffering lack of self-control. Their body isn't jerking uncontrollably, instead their life is shaking uncontrollably.

Chaos or Control?

When the Bible talks about self-control (or temperance), it includes the idea of moderation, of things done in proper balance and done in a correct way. Control makes us more effective. In sports, we usually dislike any player who is "all over the place", because they lack focus, and that lack of self-control hinders the player's ability to perform at what they are supposed to do, whether that's scoring or defending or outsmarting an opponent.

The opposite of self-control is being unfocused, abusive, chaotic, addictive, or lawless. It's the difference between the temperate life and the crazy life. Although at times that "crazy" can seem exciting, it quickly loses any appeal when we are living "crazy" every day. When we have no control, our life will be careening along in abuse of what should be good things.

Food and drink are good and essential things meant to be enjoyed, but when misused it can lead to malnutrition, obesity, alcoholism, and other abuses. Other good things people often abuse are money, sex, their own body, work, and time. If our kids get caught up in a life of chaos it will likely end badly which is why, as parents, all us would rather see our kids learn self-control.

The Flesh Life

Jesus Embraced Parenting has been focused on encouraging the fruit of the Spirit in our kids' lives, but before talking about the 9-fold fruit, Paul warns us about living the opposite life: a life that is out-of-control:

> You, my brothers and sisters, were called to be free. But do not use your freedom to indulge the flesh; rather, serve one another humbly in love. For the entire law is fulfilled in keeping this one command: "Love your neighbor as yourself." If you bite and devour each other, watch out or you will be destroyed by each other.
>
> So I say, walk by the Spirit, and you will not gratify the desires of the flesh. For the flesh desires what is contrary to the Spirit, and the Spirit what is contrary to the flesh. They are in conflict with each other, so that you are not to do whatever you want. But if you are led by the Spirit, you are not under the law.
>
> The acts of the flesh are obvious: sexual immorality, impurity and debauchery; idolatry and witchcraft; hatred, discord, jealousy, fits of rage, selfish ambition, dissensions, factions and envy; drunkenness, orgies, and the like. I warn you, as I did before, that those who live like this will not inherit the kingdom of God. (Galatians 5:13- 21 NIV)

Do we understand the truth of what Paul says? Have we taught our kids about the importance of a Spirit-led life?

The Disciplined Life

Paul shares with the people in Corinth that he'll do whatever it takes to save at least some people. He does it for the sake of the good news and wanting to share the blessing of that news. He goes on to share how serious he is about living a disciplined life:

> Do you not know that in a race all the runners run, but only one gets the prize? Run in such a way as to get the prize. Everyone who competes in the games goes into strict training. They do it to get a crown that will not last, but we do it to get a crown that will last forever. Therefore I do not run like someone running aimlessly; I do not fight like a boxer beating the air. No, I strike a blow to my body and make it my slave so that after I

have preached to others, I myself will not be disqualified for the prize. (1 Corinthians 9:24-27 NIV)

Paul's talking about controlling himself for heavenly results and to make an eternal difference in the lives of others. Wow, that is humbling.

For Heaven and Others

We are more prone to want to discipline ourselves for our own goals for "now", goals of weight loss or job promotion or wealth accumulation. Every January, gyms and weight loss groups are full of people trying to discipline themselves into better shape. Every Fall, college campuses are brimming with students who want to get that degree or certification. But then things get hard and folks drop out. They disqualify themselves. It's easy to do even when we are doing something good for ourselves.

But Paul proposes something radically different. He wants to go through all that hard work for something that won't necessarily improve us here-and-now. What an example we could be to our children if we were people who chose to discipline ourselves for the sake of heaven and others.

Daily Response

1. Have you ever lost control of yourself? What were the results?

2. How can you help your kid(s) learn self-control?

3. How can you as a parent better model self-control to your family? What are some areas where you would like to discipline yourself for the sake of heaven and others?

Sexual Integrity

The Last Holdout

Eric: I was the oddball in my teens, twenties, and thirties- the single guy who was waiting on sex until he married. I didn't date much during those years, but the girls I did date all professed similar commitments, which was vital because it really takes the willpower of two to keep out of trouble.

For the most part, my unbelieving co-workers and acquaintances grudgingly respected my commitment, even if they didn't understand it. However, there were two friends who one day mocked me for holding out, and those two were both professing Christians- one of them was even a Bible college graduate. I felt betrayed by them- guys I thought I could trust to have my back. I expected the world to not understand my desire to obey God, but I thought my Christian friends would at least be supportive. Sadly, I was wrong. Both of these guys had become sexually active, so my own commitment to sexual integrity made them uneasy. They wanted me to join them in their sin.

Seek Sexual Integrity

I don't know your sexual history and I have no desire to learn about it. But I do know that we all have our own set of baggage in this area, be it from past mistakes, lust, sexual abuse, affairs, pornography, sexual deviancy, rejections, betrayals, or even a failed marriage. One of the reasons we talk about *sexual integrity* instead of *sexual purity* is because so many of us have lost that purity/ virginity before it ought to be. But just because we faltered in sin (or it was taken from us forcefully by rape or abuse), doesn't mean that we can't live a life of integrity now.

We as parents can live that way from today onward and we can teach our kids to live that life of sexual integrity too. But they will not learn it by accident; we need to be purposeful in teaching them how, just like the Proverbs dad did so many centuries ago.

The Snare of Sexual Sin

Sometimes we think our modern days are nothing like Biblical times, but they faced the same intense temptations that we do today.

Read Proverbs 7

The Proverbs dad is warning about sexual sin and he's blunt about it. He likes to personify attributes like wisdom, knowledge, and insight, showing them as godly women worth pursuing with your whole heart. But here he personifies sexual sin as an unfaithful wife who is willing to do anything behind her husband's back to get a young man into her bed.

We meet a young man who lacks any common sense. The young guy doesn't accidentally bump into sin; he goes out looking for it.

> He was going down the street near her corner, walking along in the direction of her house at twilight, as the day was fading, as the dark of night set in. Then out came a woman to meet him, dressed like a prostitute and with crafty intent. (Proverbs 7:8-10 NIV)

I (Eric) had a pastor who liked to use the phrase, "sin makes you stupid," and that is so true. That young man thought he was sly, sneaking around her place as soon as the night arrived to hide him. But really, the "sin" was outsmarting him the whole time. He thought he was the one initiating things by going toward her place, but she was already dressed and waiting, her plans set.

We often think we are smarter than our sin. We can handle it. We are the one in charge. But really, the sin has made us too stupid to realize our own capture. When it comes to sexual sin, that entrapment can be very emotionally painful or even life-crippling. For a small few, it can even lead to criminal sexual behavior.

The Proverbs dad goes on to explain in detail how the young man is lured into sexual sin. We see spiritual things twisted for lust (v. 14). Sexual sin isn't merely passive; it boldly seeks you out (v. 15). It creates an illusion of a paradise (v. 16-18) where there will be no bad consequences (v. 19-20). Like a fishing lure to a fish, it looks so attractive that you don't even notice the hook hidden in it.

The lust pretends to be exclusive and special, but the Proverbs dad reminds his son that thousands have already gone down this road of destruction. There's nothing special or unique about our sexual sin. We might pretend it's as special as a romantic little café on a quaint side street, but it's really a crowded fast-food joint on the interstate- there are so many caught up in the same sexual sins. "Here's your order of sex with a side of passion and a big gulp of lust. Next customer!"

There's a reason why so many pornographic websites are among the world's most visited sites- this sin is addictive for us and profitable for those who are the suppliers. There's a reason why advertisers sexualize cars, beverages, food, clothing, sports, electronics, and almost everything else they are trying to sell. Lust pulls us in. Sex sells, but it also entraps.

Helping Our Children Stand Firm

Our children live in a world soaked in sex. Most likely, they've been exposed to a message of lust from ads, shows, fashion, and music. Add to that, classmates and adults who are crass or lustful. It's not pretty.

While our kids are young, we as parents can do our part to filter out as much of the junk as possible. What are we allowing into our home through television, smart phones, or the internet? Do we lock access? Do we set time limits? Are there online boundaries? Are we monitoring what they are getting exposed to by friends, cousins, or at school, because not everyone has the same morals as we do.

As our kids mature into later elementary and into the teen years, we can help them realize that to keep sexual integrity it's important to be aware of the tricks and traps that surround them. They need to be aware that there is a hook inside that pretty lure and to recognize why the lure attracts them and how the hook will snag them up. If a smart fish can realize that trap, then so can all of us- including our kids.

When Amy and I were dating, we set very specific boundaries on ourselves in order to keep our sexual integrity. (Please note: Our boundaries worked well for us, but that doesn't mean they are right for our kids or your kids. Some people will have to set far stricter boundaries on themselves, while others might be able to loosen them up. We are just sharing what worked for us.) We limited our kissing and extended hugging to only in a public and semi-public setting because we knew that getting too close when we were alone might overwhelm our intentions to wait on sex until we married. We kept our clothes on. We never took overnight trips together, which meant some late-night driving to get to separate homes after day trips to another city. We avoided movies that were too suggestive. We often did activities with others. We allowed our friends to ask brutally honest questions of us to help hold us accountable. We worked hard to respect each other and tried not to tempt each other. For us, these boundaries worked.

Now as parents ourselves, we need to find ways to help our kids hold to integrity in all aspects of their life, and especially in this area.

Daily Response

1. What are some ways you can model sexual integrity to your kids? What boundaries have you placed on yourself to maintain your own sexual integrity?

2. Our culture often jokes about parents having the "birds and bees" talk with their kids, but how would you talk to them about sexual integrity? What are some specifics you would share? What are some helpful tips for keeping to sexual integrity?

3. One of the biggest gateways into our kids' lives is through electronics, media, and online. How can we help them navigate the attacks on their sexual integrity that will come through games, shows, and online interactions?

Resisting Temptation

The Lure of Donuts

Eric: Here's a story that I've shared numerous times over the years. It's a tale about resisting sin:

Let's pretend you live in a big city where you walk to work every day. Like so many of us, you have a particular sin that you are prone to give into. Your sin is donuts. Those doughy treats are your downfall- you just can't resist them. To fight the temptation, you've purged your home of the *evil circles of sweetness*. However, along the most direct route to work, on Main Street, there is a wonderful donut shop where they make those scrumptious delicacies fresh every day. For you, it's a den of sinfulness that will overwhelm your willpower. It is a place to be avoided at all cost.

It's morning and you are feeling good today. You've had a sensible breakfast and are out the door and ready to walk to work. You know it would be best to avoid the road that passes the donut shop, but you're feeling strong today.

It won't be a problem for me, you say to yourself. *Donuts aren't that much of a temptation anymore. Besides, Main Street is the quickest route to work- so why take a longer way?*

So you start walking along Main Street. Your conscience is nagging you a bit because you know what's coming in a few blocks: that place-that-should-not-be named. To be a little careful, you decide to stay on the other side of the street, and that decision makes you feel good. It seems like a fair compromise: you're taking the fastest way to work but you're keeping a safe distance from that approaching temptation.

But as you keep walking you realize that the morning shadows are thicker over here and you start feeling more chilled with each stride. Most other walkers seem to realize the same thing, because there are a lot more pedestrians on that other sidewalk, all of them in the warm glow of early morning sunshine.

It sure looks a lot sunnier on that other side, you think to yourself. *I can walk over there like all those others without giving in to the donuts. When I get to that block, I'll look straight ahead and I won't even glance at the place. I can do this. I'm stronger than those little round puffs of perfection.*

You feel a little guilty as you cross over to the warmer sidewalk so you start walking faster, proving your resolve to keep going... at least you do until a red light stops your progress. As you wait for the light to change, you look ahead and catch a glimpse of that funny sign hanging in front of the donut shop. You've always thought that sign was a clever way to announce the place. For a brief moment you reminisce on the first time you found the shop and enjoyed that first fantastic treat. That first warm bite! Mmmm, it was heavenly...

For just a moment, you consider turning down the cross street, but then the light changes and everyone starts walking around you. You give in, and keep going up Main Street. All these hundreds of people can simply walk by the donut shop; you can too.

Next thing you know, you're standing in front of the donut shop and looking in the big window. Oh, those donuts look soooo good.

An elderly lady walks out the door with her bag of delicious donuts and with her comes that delightful smell and the warmth of the place. Oh, they smell sooo good.

You grab the door before it bangs her- after all you're just being polite- and then you slip inside. The guy behind the counter gives you a warm greeting and invites you to try a sample of their newest creation. You know that you should turn away, but it's just a nibble and it won't cost anything...

You take the sample and feel that warmth in your hand and anticipate the sweetness in your mouth. You suddenly realize that you are about to give into your greatest sin once again and you silently plea to God for help.

Unable to resist, you gobble that treat and quickly request a dozen more. As you do, you feel guilty but you also kind of blame God a little because he didn't rescue you when you called out to him.

Overwhelming Sin

Why does it seem that sin can overwhelm and overpower us? We don't want to sin again, but then we do. Sometimes it seems unfair; hundreds of others are able to walk by the donut shop without falling, why can't we? Why does that temptation of lust or greed or jealousy or lying seem so strong? Why can't we just say no to it and why doesn't God take those desires away from us?

Teaching How to Resist

When it comes to helping our kids resist temptations, it seemed easier when they were younger. When our boys were toddlers, we found it easy to help them avoid temptations by just keeping them away from situations that would tempt them.

Eric: When I was a little fellow, my mom stopped taking me into a discount store after it became obvious that I lusted for all the cheap toys and would have a tantrum if I didn't get one immediately. She avoided the store completely so she wouldn't have to face my meltdown over some lousy toy I couldn't have. Similarly, when our own kids were small, Amy and I could easily keep them away from locations or situations that were too much.

At home, we just moved the greatest temptations out of reach of our toddlers. Things moved higher and higher on the shelves as the boys went from crawling to walking to climbing. Our home decor might have looked strange, but it was an easy solution for helping our kids avoid certain temptations by simply moving the item out-of-reach.

Unfortunately, as they grow older it becomes much harder to move new temptations out of reach. We've restricted television and online access. We've monitored friendships and kept them away from situations where peer pressure might overwhelm. But as the years go by, the temptations become more complex and our ability to protect them becomes less. We are forced more into the role of advisor, trying to teach them how to recognize the temptations in their life and how to learn the skills to resist those traps successfully.

The Power of Sin

Read Romans 7 and 8

The Apostle Paul shared how he felt overwhelmed by sin himself. He wanted to do the right thing, but found himself still doing the wrong things.

> I do not understand what I do. For what I want to do I do not do, but what I hate I do. And if I do what I do not want to do, I agree that the law is good. As it is, it is no longer I myself who do it, but it is sin living in me. For I know that good itself does not dwell in me, that is, in my sinful nature. For I have the desire to do what is good, but I cannot carry it out. For I do not do the good I want to do, but the evil I do not want to do—this I keep on doing. Now if I do what I do not want to do, it is no longer I who do it, but it is sin living in me that does it.
>
> So I find this law at work: Although I want to do good, evil is right there with me. For in my inner being I delight in God's law; but I see another law at work in me, waging war against the law of my mind and making me a prisoner of the law of sin at work within me. What a wretched man I am! Who will rescue me from this body that is subject to death? Thanks be to God, who delivers me through Jesus Christ our Lord!
>
> So then, I myself in my mind am a slave to God's law, but in my sinful nature a slave to the law of sin. (Romans 7:15-25 NIV)

The Power of the Spirit

For Paul, the temptation was overwhelming and he didn't find a solution until he discovered the freeing empowerment from Jesus. In Chapter 8, he shares it is the Spirit who gives life and set him free. That Jesus, through his sacrifice for our sins, gives us the ability to live a new life controlled by the Spirit rather than our sinful desires.

> Therefore, there is now no condemnation for those who are in Christ Jesus, because through Christ Jesus the law of the Spirit who gives life has set you free from the law of sin and death. For what the law was powerless to do because it was weakened by the flesh, God did by sending his own Son in the likeness of sinful flesh to be a sin offering. And so he condemned sin in the flesh, in order that the righteous requirement of the law might be fully met in us, who do not live according to the flesh but according to the Spirit. (Romans 8:1-4 NIV)

So we can have victory over temptation, whether that temptation is a donut or a discount-store toy, whether its pornography or envy or rage or lying or gossiping or any of a hundred other wrongful desires. We can beat this, by leaning on Jesus. We resist temptation by our choice of lifestyle. If we live according to the Spirit rather than living for the temptations, then we'll have success. It is a choice on our part. It is a choice for our kids too.

We usually don't have victory over sin when we've been playing with that sin for awhile. When our nose is already pressed up against that bakery case or when we are halfway through a questionable movie we are too late to resist. When we've already listened to a gossiper for 30 minutes or we've been brooding all morning over some slight a co-worker gave us, we've already fed our habits of gossip or rage and they will soon explode in size.

Resisting temptation needs to start earlier, before we start walking to work (in the donut shop story) or before we pick which store we will shop at. We need to admit our weaknesses and choose to follow the Holy Spirit instead of our wrongful desires. We need to learn how to resist and we need to teach our kids those same skills.

Finally, Paul gave us these words of encouragement when we face temptation:

> No temptation has overtaken you except what is common to mankind. And God is faithful; he will not let you be tempted beyond what you can bear. But when you are tempted, he will also provide a way out so that you can endure it. (1 Corinthians 10: 13 NIV)

Daily Response

1. What is a sin that you've had to work hard to resist? Why has that sin been tough for you?

2. What has helped you to succeed in resisting temptations?

3. What sins have you seen your kids being tempted by? How can you help them to learn how to resist?

Peer Pressure

Trying to Buy Friends

Amy: As an elementary kid, I had a set of wooden letters that were custom made for me. I gave them to another girl in the neighborhood to buy her friendship. (My attempted bribe ended when my mom realized what I had done and made me get those wooden letters back.)

Over my 20+ years as a school teacher, I've seen a lot of similar pressure among students, whether elementary aged or middle schooler. One example that I've seen repeated so many times, is a kid (often a new girl just transferred to the school) trying to buy friends with gifts. They bring stuffies, jewelry, candy, and lots of other trinkets and then give them to others, hoping to become their friends. The problem is the giving pressure never stops. Those "friends" keep wanting more and more, and then they desert the girl when the gifts run out. Inevitably, I'm consoling a crying girl. The drama of it all, and it's caused by the pressure to fit in and be liked.

Trying to Fit In

Who hasn't felt the pressure to fit in? Many of the struggles we faced growing up are much the same as the struggles our kids face today. Although technology is more advanced and maybe society seems worse than ever, the peer pressures are much the same as they were decades ago. This fact should help us have more compassion and understanding for our children.

The pressure might come from a stranger over the Internet rather than from the teen that lives down the street, but they are still similar to what we faced growing up ourselves. All of us have faced (or are facing now) the pressure to fit in, be liked, be accepted, be respected, be popular, be successful (whatever that means at a particular age), or be loved. That pressure can even lead to harmful or illegal activities as we try to please other people rather trying to please God with our choices.

Facing Peer Pressure

Kids will face peer pressure almost constantly during their years of growing up- pressure on who to hang out with, what to like or dislike, and what to wear, watch, or listen to. Just the other day, our 3rd Grader reported that a kid in his class ate a crayon and some paper on a dare.

Our kids will be enticed to "have a little fun" to "try it" to do what "everyone is doing." The dares and temptations can get more dangerous as our kids get older. That peer pressure could lead to injury, jail, pregnancy, addiction, or even death.

As an example, the Proverbs Dad realizes that his son will be pressured to join one of the gangs that are robbing and even murdering to get loot. He gives a sober warning:

> Listen, my son, to your father's instruction
> and do not forsake your mother's teaching.
> They are a garland to grace your head
> and a chain to adorn your neck.
> My son, if sinful men entice you,
> do not give in to them.
> If they say, "Come along with us;
> let's lie in wait for innocent blood,
> let's ambush some harmless soul;
> let's swallow them alive, like the grave,
> and whole, like those who go down to the pit;
> we will get all sorts of valuable things
> and fill our houses with plunder;
> cast lots with us;
> we will all share the loot"—
> my son, do not go along with them,
> do not set foot on their paths;
> for their feet rush into evil,
> they are swift to shed blood.
> How useless to spread a net
> where every bird can see it!
> These men lie in wait for their own blood;
> they ambush only themselves!
> Such are the paths of all who go after ill-gotten gain;
> it takes away the life of those who get it.
> (Proverbs 1:8-19 NIV)

Hopefully, your kids aren't being tempted to join a violent gang, but they are very likely being tempted into some kind of sin by their peers. It might be a temptation to lie, gossip, lust, drunkenness, hatred, envy, bragging, or any number of other things. A preschooler might be tempted to join another in a lie so that neither of them gets in trouble. A teen might be tempted by drugs or sex or thievery. The peer pressure to "join in" will happen, no matter the age of our kid. It doesn't help when society is encouraging them to sin as well (and we all know that most ads and entertainment feed into some kind of sin, making it look like something fun without any bad consequences).

The Proverbs Dad gives some sound advice to his son on how he can avoid peer pressure that we can also apply to our own child:

1. **Do not give in to them** (v. 10) Friends and classmates will try to entice you, making it sound so wonderful, but stand firm against it. They'll try shaming you, bullying you, or even bribing you to join. Don't give in.

2. **Do not go along with them** (v.15) You might be tempted to just stay with them as they get into trouble, telling yourself that you won't do it yourself even while they are, but no one can hold out for long as just a watcher. You are a witness to their wrongs- either it will offend you and drive you away or it will slowly lure you to try it yourself. If what they are doing is illegal, then you have become an accessory to the crime and you can still be prosecuted for not stopping their actions. Don't go along with them.

3. **Don't set foot on their paths** (v. 15) You might be tempted to follow along afterwards, not wanting to be left too far behind. Maybe you just want to see what has happened. You aren't right in the middle of it, but you are following behind. Maybe you're catching up after they've gotten high or after they've stolen from the market or after they've mocked or beaten someone. You arrive later, but you're still on their "path" and you can see what damage it's doing to them and to their victims- but only if you're willing to be honest and look.

Positive Pressure

Peer pressure can also be a positive thing, but that is rarer. Society usually won't encourage such things, so we as parents need to encourage our kids to apply pressure towards positive, healthy, creative, and spiritual things. As parents, we can try to make our home a hub for good fun where our kids and their friends can laugh and create. We can also encourage our kids to make a positive difference in our community, from volunteering at a food pantry, to tutoring younger kids, to cleaning up hiking trails.

We can encourage sports, clubs, volunteering at church, learning new skills, or anything else our child is interested in. We can and should apply positive pressure on our kids to explore their talents and to excel at them.

Even greater, we should encourage our kids to please God foremost, rather than wanting to please other people. Where people are fickle and society's expectations seem to morph to something different every year, God doesn't change. What God desires from our children is the same every year, every decade. The more we teach our kids to know God and follow him, the easier it will be for them to stand up to bad peer pressure. It is no guarantee to escaping peer pressure, but the Holy Spirit can certainly help them.

Daily Response

1. Think back to your own childhood. What are some of the peer pressures that you experienced?

2. What are some of the peer pressures that your child is facing now?

3. How can you help your child learn how to resist peer pressure?

4. What are positive activities that your child could do instead of giving in to particular pressures?

WEEK 9   **DAY 5**

Putting on our New Nature

Overpowered by Sin

Amy and Eric: Before we were believers, we couldn't help but sin, no matter how good we tried to be. Amy came to Christ at an early age (6), while Eric came to Christ during his senior year in high school at 18.

Did we both face the same daunting temptations before we came to Jesus? Yes and no. A six-year-old isn't tempted with the exact same things that a teen is, but at the root the sins are still much the same: selfishness, greed, fear, deceit, anger and so on.

Before Jesus, we had no real power to resist. Sin had us chained, whether we realized it or not.

Jesus Set Us Free

Every single person born on this planet has a sin nature. We've all sinned, so we might as well admit it. We were all captives to sin, no matter our age or circumstances.

That's why Jesus came. He came to set us free from the behavior we couldn't stop on our own. He came to pay the penalty for our sin by dying on the cross. Three days later, he rose again, defeating death itself. We just need to embrace him and his offer to us. As Paul wrote, "If you declare with your mouth, 'Jesus is Lord,' and believe in your heart that God raised him from the dead, you will be saved." (Romans 10:9 NIV)

Because of what Jesus did for us, we can now have the ultimate self-control. We can now choose to follow him, but what does it look like to follow Jesus?

Replacing the Old with the New

Following Jesus can't be done without his remaking us and his Spirit empowering us.

> Therefore, if anyone is in Christ, the new creation has come: The old has gone, the new is here! All this is from God, who reconciled us to himself through Christ and gave us the ministry of reconciliation: that God

221

was reconciling the world to himself in Christ, not counting people's sins against them. And he has committed to us the message of reconciliation. We are therefore Christ's ambassadors, as though God were making his appeal through us. We implore you on Christ's behalf: Be reconciled to God. God made him who had no sin to be sin for us, so that in him we might become the righteousness of God (2 Corinthians 5: 17-21 NIV)

You were taught, with regard to your former way of life, to put off your old self, which is being corrupted by its deceitful desires; to be made new in the attitude of your minds; and to put on the new self, created to be like God in true righteousness and holiness.
(Ephesians 4: 22-24 NIV)

As a new creation in Christ, we are no longer slaves to sin:

For those who are led by the Spirit of God are the children of God. The Spirit you received does not make you slaves, so that you live in fear again; rather, the Spirit you received brought about your adoption to sonship. And by him we cry, "Abba, Father." The Spirit himself testifies with our spirit that we are God's children. Now if we are children, then we are heirs—heirs of God and co-heirs with Christ, if indeed we share in his sufferings in order that we may also share in his glory. (Romans 8:14-17 NIV)

Best News Ever: Jesus has set us free!

We have been set free in Jesus. Really, totally free. We are now able to say "yes" to so many good things. Through the empowerment of the Spirit, we finally are able to control ourselves and are able to choose to do things that really matter now and for eternity.

- We can choose to be loved and in turn love others
- We can fight off sin and choose righteousness
- We can submit to the Holy Spirit
- We can accept the love of God
- We can teach our kids how to serve Jesus rather than serve mere humans
- We can be the parents that God has called us to be

Daily Response

1. Have you experienced the freedom Jesus has promised? Why or why not?

2. Does your child know Jesus and the freedom he provides? What convinces you of that opinion?

3. How can you model living in the new nature to your child?

Gathering ending Week 9
Notes

SPECIAL EVENT

As a final activity of this 10-week experience, we ask that you commit to the following pledge as a public commitment before the rest of the group and also show it to your children:

Parent Pledge

I,_____ as a parent and a follower of Jesus, take personal responsibility to do the following:

- Teach my child about Jesus and the salvation He offers
- Pray *for* my child and **with** my child regularly
- Nurture the fruits of the Spirit in my child by teaching what it means to submit to the Lord's working in us to bring forth love, joy, peace, patience, kindness, goodness, faithfulness, gentleness and self-control
- Model the Christian walk to my child by demonstrating the fruits of the Spirit in my own life

Signed:_____

Date:_____

(To download a printable copy of the Parental Pledge, please visit the Jesus Embraced website at https://jesusembraced.org/forms)

Jesus Embraced PARENTING

GROUP LEADER GUIDE

a group Bible study by

ERIC and AMY LORENZEN

Ready to lead your own Jesus Embraced group?
If so, be sure to get our **Group Leader Guide.**

Looking for another great Bible study?

Jesus
Embraced

Bible studies to bring us closer

"Warm and personable. Like sitting down and talking with friends."
(praise for *Jesus Embraced Parenting*)

Visit JesusEmbraced.org to learn more about our studies.
https://jesusembraced.org/